VALIANT THOR'S
BOOK OF RELATIONSHIPS

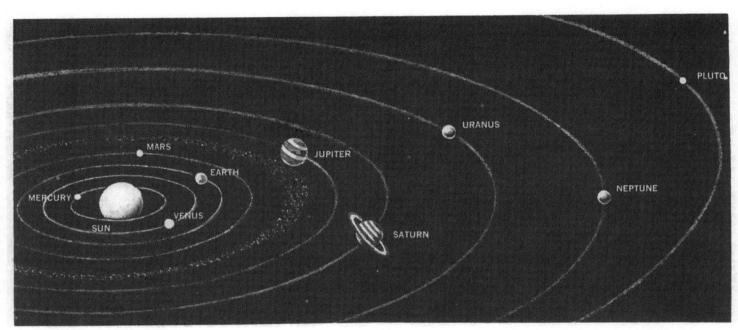

NASA

THE SOLAR SYSTEM

VALIANT THOR'S
BOOK OF RELATIONSHIPS
LOVE, HEALTH, AND SUCCESS THROUGH INTERPLANETARY AWARENESS

VALIANT THOR

BOOK OF RELATIONSHIPS
ISBN-13: 978-1539905127
ISBN-10: 1539905128

PRINTING HISTORY
Saucerian edition published 1966
New Age Press edition published 1984
New Saucerian edition published 2016

©2016 New Saucerian Press

DEDICATED

To all of Earth's People

.....Adoni Vasu

Introduction

"HAVE SPACE PEOPLE COMMUNICATED WITH EARTH?"

That was the headline on an advertisement we inserted in the Fall, 1966, issue of SAUCER NEWS, the excellent publication issued by Mr. James W. Moseley.

"A well known researcher," our ad continued, "announces communication with people on all known planets in our solar system -- as well as the undiscovered ones! We are not permitted to publish the name of this researcher, since he or she does not wish to interrupt research to answer the volume of mail which would result from this article."

This researcher, through an intermediary, had sent us some little booklets, alleged to contain communications from people on other planets. The intermediary asked if I could distribute some of the booklets to people who I thought would be interested in reading the revelations.

I replied back that I would be glad to send some of them out, but was taken aback when the Express Company soon brought me about 500 pounds of them!

I hesitated to send them out undiscriminately; anyhow I couldn't afford the postage and handling costs on such a quantity. Then some people just didn't believe the other planets were inhabited and probably would react negatively if they received the booklets.

So I held a conference with James Moseley the next time I was in New York and he agreed to donate a full page ad, since the idea was non-commercial.

So I ran the ad, offering to send the books to any subscriber who would send a few cents postage and packing fee for each booklet. The results were overwhelming. Most everybody ordered all the books, which effected economies in shipping.

The result was that I made a sizable profit on the ad, instead of losing money in distributing the books.

I took the money I had made in distributing the books from Moseley's ad and paid for an expensive ad in FATE magazine, making the same offer, being sure that the small profits left over from the multiple orders would pay for the ad.

But I hadn't figured on a sudden policy of SAUCER NEWS. Moseley made an appearance on a very popular New York TV show and offered free copies of a back issue of his magazine. Thousands of people wrote in. He sent out another printing of the issue containing the ad. Result: another huge response to my ad.

I had hoped to get some additional copies of the booklets but the original publisher could no longer affort to order another big printing. What to do about my FATE ad and the people who were answering the SAUCER NEWS ad who would be disappointed.

I made a sudden decision. I couldn't afford to reprint the books separately, but if I combined them all in one binding, in regular 8½ x 11" book form, I could send this edition out in lieu of the books.

The result is the volume you are now reading.

It, instead of the booklets, is being sent to the people who answered my FATE ad which I was unable to stop because of the deadlines, which are far in advance of publication date.

And now, something about the contents of this amazing volume. I don't know quite what to personally think of it. As I understand it, these messages were received through "psychic channeling." Some of you "buy" this; some of you do not.

Regardless of how this information was received I think it is very interesting. The messages also contain thoughts of high moral content and are certainly uplifting. While I would much prefer to believe messages received on regular radio wave lengths, I am not going to try to discredit information received by psychic means.

Many people wrote asking if there were a book about Mars. I had planned to add some material on Mars, possibly from other psychic channeling sources; but upon re-reading the material I learned in one of the other chapters that the first section of the book, "THE BOOK OF SPACESHIPS," is allegedly by a Martian and is about Mars.

We do hope that you find the contents of this book interesting and helpful. We would particularly like to hear from you after you read it, and to get your reactions. We would like to know if readers of our various books would like us to continue occasional publication of this type of book (similar to the former EXTRATERRESTRIAL COMMUNICATION) which was well received. While we personally do not prefer this kind of book, we want to present ALL NEW AGE IDEAS.

Please do not ask us to tell you the source of this material, for we are still carrying out our original promise not to reveal this information.

Gray Barker, 1966

NOTE TO THE 1984 EDITION: In the "It Can Now Be Told" Dept., we must reveal that we were aided in this endeavor by the illustrious Venusian, Valiant Thor (reputed to be the tutor of Tesla), who was kind enough to write to us after his escape from the Pentagon in 1966. That emotionally charged material became the seed for this book, and can be found in the first chapter, "Earth-Space Relationships."

Since I still did not have enough material for a book, Thor suggested we describe the qualities of the various planets in human terms, so that people could better understand how their lives are influenced by the planets - intertwined.

The whole thing turned out to be a kind of intergalactic performance art piece, with Thor playing the role of each planet - not too hard for him, given his knowledge of interplanetary civilizations and modes of communication. (Thor is a lover of art, who has been known to frequent New York City art events.)

THE AGE OF SPACE

If there has been a single factor responsible for our success over the past two hundred years, it has been the characteristic American confidence in the future. It was such a confidence which brought the first colonists westward across the Atlantic to settle the Eastern shores. It was that same confidence which brought other generations westward across the continent to build up our country all the way to the Pacific.

Today there are those who argue that we should not push forward into new realms or new enterprises except when there is clear evidence of competition from other nations. I believe the American people reject the concept that their future shall be measured by the reaction to accomplishments of others.

America's commitment to the exploration of space for peaceful purposes is a firm commitment. We will not retreat from our national purpose. We will not be turned aside in our national effort by those who would attempt to divert us.

Our national purpose in space is peace—not just prestige.

—PRESIDENT LYNDON B. JOHNSON.

Contents

INTRODUCTION 7

THE EARTH-SPACE RELATIONSHIP 13

FROM PLANET PLUTO WITH BROTHERLY LOVE 23

NEPTUNE FROM EXPERIENCE GIVES ADVICE 31

URANUS LOVER OF MAN SPEAKS 35

SATURN PLANET OF PEACE SENDS WARNING 41

FROM JUPITER THE PLANET OF JOY 49

INVITATION FROM THE PLANET VENUS 53

PLANET MERCURY SENDS GREETINGS 59

THREE UNDISCOVERED PLANETS 67

The Earth-Space Relationship

There has been the need for a book of this kind for some time. The world of humanity has been aroused by reports of what they at first called flying saucers, because in the sky the light struck them in such a way that they appeared to be round, like a saucer, and they were moving so fast a good view could not be had of them. More recently it has been seen that some of them are quite large and long in shape, like a ship, not round like a saucer.

But still they are mysterious objects to the inhabitants of the planet Earth, and there has been both fear and scientific interest expressed in regard to them. The answer to all questions is very simple, especially now that mankind has developed flying ships of their own. These are air ships from other planets. But the question has remained, why are they coming over the earth, are their designs sinister, or are they friendly? For a long time there was only fear expressed, because the people of Earth had become so accustomed to wars between nations, that war was the first thought in their minds. How sad this is, and entirely contrary to the truth.

Some of us have managed to contact certain members of the human race, who were of high intelligence, and whose minds were eager to know the truth and the reason for these ships of the air descending so close to the planet Earth. Some of our Space Craft have landed, and we have managed to talk with some of the more spiritually evolved members of the human race, but the vast majority of men are still worried when they hear of these ships.

It is the hope of the writer of this book, that all fear may be overcome by a presentation of the true situation by one who really knows at first hand, being a traveler in space ships, as well as an aerial traveler without any kind of vehicle but his own body. I am that kind of Being, and am the Ruler of a Planet near the earth. Every planet has a Ruler, and the name that is used for the Ruler may shock some of the devoutly religious of Earth, who do not understand. We are called Gods, and there is one for each planet.

The human race has believed for eons of time that their planet was the only one inhabited. When men looked up into the sky and saw the shining stars, the moon, and sun, they thought that all these beautiful objects were created for the benefit of the people of earth, and were comparatively small objects, as they seemed to be, to the naked eye of man. Even now when marvelous telescopes have been invented, man knows very little about the planets which appear in his telescope.

So before we enter into the subject of space ships, it is necessary to discuss planets. Space ships are used for travel between the planets, so now we shall study the planets—only those of the solar system in which the earth is a planet. Each planet is a small part of the solar system, and the solar system is only one of many solar systems, which all together make the universe. The universe is only one of many universes, which all together are beyond the imagining of the mind of man.

Close your eyes, relax, and try to imagine anything extending in all directions without any ending. This is the universe of universes. How small and insignificant is a solar system in comparison, and how extremely small is one planet of a solar system. What we are now concerning ourselves with, is the planet Earth and its sister planets.

All the planets are globes, as is the earth, but the globes vary greatly in size. There are many which are very much larger than the little planet Earth. Mars, Jupiter, Venus, to mention a few. Astronomers, at the present time, are learning much about the planets that they never knew before, but it is still comparatively little. The distances between the planets is not very great, and can be easily traveled by space ships, which are very much more advanced inventions than the airplanes of the earth. They are noiseless, and their power is derived from the atmosphere, and is pure and without odor.

For centuries man has believed his Earth to be the only inhabited planet. Certain conditions of warmth, moisture, soil, etc., were considered necessary for the life of any being resembling man or animal. He has made two mistakes. In the first place, all living creatures do not need the same conditions that man does; in the second place, man's scientific instruments do not accurately register the conditions that prevail on each planet.

The truth is, that almost every planet is inhabited by beings very similar to man. There also is vegetable and animal life. In fact, few of the planets are barren and uninhabitable.

Besides this, many of them have civilizations which far surpass that of any nation on the earth. It is known by your historians that there have been civilizations on earth that have fallen and disappeared. Archaeologists are now making discoveries which show that there were marvelously advanced civilizations on the earth, which for one reason or another were destroyed, and disappeared from the face of the earth. Their marvelous cities are being uncovered, and much is being learned about the lives of those ancient peoples.

Wonderful civilizations like these are now flourishing on many of the planets in this solar system. There are some more backward than the Earth, but they are few. The majority are equal to the Earth, or in advance of it. Man has begun to question, "Why should the Earth be the only inhabited planet?" The answer is, it is not.

Now man is endeavoring to obtain information concerning the planet Mars and the moon. There is much talk about the atmosphere of the moon, and the soil. Some scientists say the soil is only dry dust, which is blown about by the wind. Others contradict this and say it is rich and could be productive. All study is for the purpose of using the moon as a defense base from which to hurl bombs on the enemy. How sad this is! Instead of living together in peace, harmony and brotherly love, the human race, in all parts of the Earth, is either fighting with physical weapons, or competing with one another for the gaining of wealth and luxury. It is all fighting and war though different kinds.

How different it is on the planets in the neighborhood of the Earth, those of whose inhabitants the Earth people are so much afraid. They judge only by themselves, and therefore believe the inhabitants of these planets to be warlike and greedy, as they are. So when occasionally a space ship is seen, it is assumed that its purpose is to harm the inhabitants of earth.

This writing is for the purpose of dispelling this erroneous idea. We are reaching out the hand of friendship and man believes it is holding a bomb. Instead of this it is an offer of information and assistance in the building of space craft, for ours are far in advance of the noisy, clumsy, flying ships of the planet Earth. The few understanding ones of Earth would be pleased to have our cooperation and would pass our information to the others who are of a scientific turn of mind.

The first thing is to learn how to use the energy that is in the atmosphere. This runs our ships and is always available without cost. The next thing is to learn to make the craft a somewhat different shape than the present airplanes. The present planes are beautiful as they fly high in the air looking like great dragon flies sailing with spread wings, but the shape of our ships is much more practical for the purpose for which they are used—flight.

But the very first thing to accomplish is to overcome man's suspicious attitude and win the trust and friendship of humanity.

This must be done by spiritual teaching, and the knowledge of our philosophy, which is more than philosophy to discuss and exercise the mind on, it is the breath of life to us and we practice and live it. I shall now explain this knowledge.

It is very much like the New Age teaching of the earth. This New Age teaching is Truth, but only a comparatively small number of the people study it, and not all of them practice it. We believe with all our hearts that there is a Mighty Power, invisible to all eyes, that is the cause of all life and the sustainer of it.

We do not give It the name of God, we call It Life Eternal. We feel Its Presence all around us, in us and acting through us. I am one of those we call Gods. We are very advanced in the art of living. We are able to perform miracles, as you call them. These are all natural phenomena. We who are Gods do not need space ships for our travels, we can move rapidly through space by the forces that are in our bodies. And we do not need to move in order to see, hear and know all that takes place everywhere.

Each planet has a God who has created the planet. It is so of the Earth. You people of Earth have a wonderful God who has created the planet Earth He loves all His creation just as we all do. It has been said, God is Love and that is true of all Gods. All the planets near the earth have Gods of love and the inhabitants of the planets in turn love their Gods with all their hearts, minds and strength.

It would be impossible for the people of these planets to deliberately injure any living being. They all live lives of love and joy, for true love is joy. No one who feels that love and joy could ever hurt another living thing. This is what we are trying to make man understand. If mankind would drop their destructive ways, they too would live lives of love and joy, without conflict of any kind. All would be peace and plenty.

Oh, if man would only understand and he shall understand after reading this book and others, which shall tell of the experiences of enlightened men, who have seen the space ships and talked with those who came to Earth in them. These illumined ones have had great trouble in making their fellow men believe their reports of their experiences. Man is notably reluctant to accept any new belief or idea, he clings tenaciously to his old established beliefs and practices.

But this shall soon change, for the pressure of Truth is becoming too great to be resisted. It is not very long now, as time is measured, before mankind will accept the fact that there are other inhabited planets, and the fact that the inhabitants of those planets near the Earth not only can visit the Earth, but are visiting the Earth. More persons will be seeing the space craft and, as the old human saying goes, "seeing is believing."

That has been the great trouble with humanity, they have put greater reliance on their physical eyes than on their mental understanding. It is well known that the report of the eyes cannot be accepted as it seems to be. A trite example is, the railroad tracks do not come closer together in the distance. Investigation and knowledge has proven that fact. Investigation and knowledge must be applied to every new experience, no matter what it may be, whether pleasant and desirable or unpleasant. The truth should be searched for and when found accepted. Turning the back and looking away from a fact, will not change or remove it.

Enough persons have encountered space ships from other planets and talked with those in them to make it an established fact. Now the next thing to do is to investigate and find out what and who they are, and why they are visiting the planet Earth. This writing is a simple and frank presentation of the truth of the situation, but man must investigate with an open mind and find the truth of the matter for himself.

The question is, how to do that. It is simple to answer. Most of the ships have been appearing in the United States of America, for this is the country most able to follow directions in building these craft. It will require money and skilled scientists to build them. The method of drawing the power from the atmosphere is not difficult, but it requires scientific minds to understand it. There are plenty of such minds in this great country. But there are not so many minds that are without prejudice.

It is strange, but it is a fact, that brilliant and well educated scientists are among the slowest people to accept a new thought or idea. It is a rule with them to accept no new concept until it has been proven. But how can it be proven, if it is shut out without investigation just because it is new? How strangely the minds of even the most intelligent men can act. It is said that Diogenes went about with a lantern searching for an honest man. So we might search for an unprejudiced man. It is indeed rare to find any member of the human race, man, woman or child entirely without prejudice. However we do find some who will listen to reason, and who can be persuaded to finally accept new concepts. It is our hope that one scientist may be found, who is intelligent to a high degree and without strong prejudice. We have faith that this shall be.

Besides these two qualifications there is a third that is necessary; he must be able to receive instruction spiritually by telepathy. That is the way this writing is being done; some call it dictation in the mind. The communication between giver and receiver is very close. It is often so close that the one receiving believes he is thinking, and the words are his own. He has no knowledge that another mind from another dimension of life is speaking into his mind.

Man calls this inspiration. Musicians and painters are inspired in this way, by impressions received from higher dimensions, which are above the ordinary man's understanding. This communication is very easy between planets of this solar system. We feel sure that we shall find a scientist of this type whom we can inspire in the invention of a space ship similar to ours. It will be new to him, but it will not be really new.

All originates in the One Great Source, which is expressing everywhere, in everything. This Great Source is Life, and from It flows Life in every expression. We who are called Gods are expressions of Life, which flows from the One Great Source, and takes form.

I shall give myself as an example. I created this planet and breathed the breath of Life into all the inhabitants, whom I also formed. But the power and ability to do this were not mine, I received the power and knowledge from the One Great Source. This is what Jesus meant when he said, "Of myself I can do nothing, it is the Father within me who doeth the works."

That is the truth of all Life in one sentence. I say the same of myself, for acting in and through me is a higher Being, and above and in him is a higher Being than he, and so on back to the Great Source of all Life. All the planets, solar systems, and universes were created in this way. You who are reading this were created in this way. Nothing was created in any other way. Life originated in the One Great Source, which had no beginning, and shall have no end. We cannot imagine what It is like, it is beyond our imagination. We only know that It is, and that without It nothing would be.

The space ships were created in this way, and in this way man can create them if he so desires. For desire is a necessary step in the creation of anything. Without desire nothing comes into existence. Strong, steady, unwavering desire is a must in all creation. It must be without doubt. There must be a sureness of accomplishment that nothing can shake.

That is the way man has evolved and unfolded. That is the way the lower forms of life have evolved. They do not reason, they do not think as man does, but within them is an unconscious desire for something more. They change from a lower form to a higher, more complex form, with a higher state of consciousness. By a strong desire man can accomplish anything, for it is not he who accomplishes, but the power of the Great Source of Life that is in him, and in all that is. Without Life nothing could take form and be active.

So we of the planets near the Earth offer our assistance to the Earth, but without the desire and acceptance of man nothing can be accomplished. With desire there must be love for that which is desired. Love is the source of all creation. One must love ones work in order to be successful. All great scientists love their work. They will devote many hours, without rest or sleep, when they feel that something is being accomplished, or about to be brought to light. Those persons who work only for money are weary before the day is over.

So in order for us to give man the secret of our space craft, we must find at least one scientist of the highest caliber, who can receive that which we have to give. How joyfully we shall give instruction when it is desired. How much love we shall pour into the work along with our knowledge. Our space ships can be copied, or perhaps even improved. Who knows?

Intercourse between the Earth and the other planets is the result which will follow the construction of these ships of the air. From visits to the other planets man will see how life can be lived in brotherly love, and what joy, peace and plenty, both spiritual and physical, will result when love rules instead of force.

Oh beloved ones of the Earth, our hearts ache when we see the misery, poverty, and greed upon the Earth. All is force and struggle. With us all is peace and harmony. It is our strong desire to see the people of Earth living also in love, with plenty of material gifts for all, nature responding to the love that will fill the atmosphere. Our love we send to you, our help we offer to you, we pray it be accepted. If man could only see our beautiful planets and realize that the same beauty, joy and peace could be his on the planet Earth, he would surely make every effort to attain this wonderful joy and peace.

It is the peace of God which passeth understanding. It is in the center of every living being, ready to come forth into the outer life. This it cannot do in the midst of hatred and selfishness. In divine love there is the peace which will revolutionize the world of man. It may seem that I repeat this too often, but repetition is necessary in order to anchor the point in the minds of mankind.

Now you have been told what to do and what not to do, the next thing is how to do it. It has been said, and rightly, that one cannot love to order, love is spontaneous. Yes, but it can be brought forth by acting in the way love calls for. Do unto others as you would have them do to you. This does not mean for the purpose of having them do the same to you. No, it is simply a gauge for action, and when this is practiced love will follow. Be honest in all your dealings, give a little more rather than a little less. This old motto means exactly what it states, there is no return promised. But there is a return after practicing this for some time; love will be felt for the ones one has dealings with, and they, subconsciously will feel that love and return it.

This is the recipe for peace on earth, goodwill toward men. You upon the earth have just celebrated the birth of your beloved Master Jesus who loves all mankind with a love that transcends all darkness, and brings the light into all hearts and minds that will open to receive it. During the time of Christmas much love flows forth from the hearts of mankind. The giving and receiving of presents is done in love and peace and little children are especially recipients of this love and joy.

Oh, if this blessed time could be always, what a different place the Earth would be. Peace would replace battle, love would replace selfish greed. This is what the other planets wish to help the Earth people to attain and keep. There is some love now, and the problem is to expand it, to make it flow out in all directions with depth and sincerity.

We believe that visits to her sister planets; tours of inspection; conversations with the inhabitants; visits of a week or more in order to make friends; would open the eyes, hearts and minds of the inhabitants of Earth so that they would desire to follow our example.

Desire is the first step in any accomplishment. A strong, eager desire will be followed by an effort to learn how to attain that which is desired. This will be followed by action. With love in the heart for the Great Source of all Life, Love and Peace from which all blessings flow, humanity will become one with the similar beings on the other planets in this solar system.

There are many more solar systems, but love begins at home and from there goes out to other systems beyond us. As I have said before, much depends upon your scientists. Most of you will be astonished to hear that already there are scisentists on the earth who are receiving instruction from our planet—the one on which I dwell. They do not yet know that what comes to them as inspiration is coming from scientists of another planet.

Some of the more spiritually minded ones realize that they are in communication with a higher source, but they do not know that the source is another planet. They will be informed of this soon now, for everything on the earth is being speeded up. The spiritual atmosphere is being purified and the light is beginning to drive out the darkness. There will soon be a great upheaval all over the planet Earth. This is unavoidable.

In order to let the good come in the evil must be driven out, the two cannot exist together. Selfishness must disappear and love can then enter in. But, and this seems strange and contradictory, the cleansing must be done with love. The vigorous action hurts and destroys, but the vigorous action of cleansing comes from pure, divine love. This is beginning on the earth now and will continue for some time, growing stronger and more painful.

The dwellers on my planet are not taking any part in the cleansing, this is, as you might say "none of our business." Our work is to help in the reconstruction that will follow the cleansing, and as has been already stated, we are now inspiring, helping, and informing those spiritually able to receive our communications.

This book is one of our means of communication. It is intended to reach many thousands of people, who are ready to receive information if it is simply and clearly stated, and above all, honest. This book is all of that and we know that it will receive a hearty welcome.

My love and blessing is in every word; the love and blessing of the one who writes is in every word; and the love and blessing of all my people is in every word; for they know that this is being written. Those who read it will feel that love, even though it may be unconsciously, and it will give them understanding, and warm their hearts.

So, as you read, you are receiving benefit both mentally and physically, for my vibrations are flowing from the atmosphere around this book all through your being. The publishers and the printer also have received these vibrations, and have added to them their own, which are high. This is true of all spiritual books, but few persons know this.

What marvelous times are coming after the cleansing period is over on your dear planet Earth. After the cleansing period, which will be a time of great suffering and anguish, the skies will clear, the Sun Righteousness will shine over all the Earth and the Great God of Earth will reign supreme. Every human being will feel the Life and Love from the Great Source of Being active within his human form. The Christ Self will speak and act in everyone.

But since man has been given free will up to a certain point, the time of the coming of this release from misery and entrance into pure joy depends on man himself. His mind must be cleared of misconceptions and his heart must be filled with love. We of the planets near the Earth can help him to replace the misconceptions with Truth, and that will bring love into his heart.

The first step to take is to let all the inhabitants of Earth know who we are and why we are visiting the Earth in our space ships. Some already know this and are heart and soul desirous of receiving us and hearing what we have to tell them. This is a focal point from which the knowledge will spread in all directions. It is already spreading. Groups of people on the Earth have come together for the sole purpose of making contact with our ships and receiving the message of those on them. This has been accomplished by means of tape recorders. Before this there were instances of ships landing on the Earth and communication being made with individuals who were open minded and eager to receive them. Books were written and something was accomplished in arousing interest, but it did not spread far enough or fast enough. Something more had to be done and now is being done.

We have been able to go close to the Earth and our messages are received on tape recorders. These tapes can be mailed to great distances; other tapes can be made from them and sent out in other directions, and so the information is really spreading.

Now the doubters have raised a question that is a very reasonable one. How can those from other planets speak the language of the people they contact, without foreign accent, as easily and smoothly as a native. Surely they do not all speak English on the other planets. These tapes must be made by words spoken by dishonest individuals on the earth.

This is a reasonable question and the answer is simple. We on the other planets do not have to learn a new language word for word as you do on Earth. Even you Earth people have some persons who have what are called photographic memories. They remember what they have read, a whole page at a time, not by hearing but by sight. When they return home from a sightseeing trip of weeks duration they remember it all as pictures in their mind, unfolding one after another in sequence. Musicians remember the printed notes and the sounds of whole symphonies; singers remember both words and music. Your babies do not come into the world talking, they learn by listening to the adults and older children around them.

Now you understand how we are able

to speak your languages without difficulty. We come close enough so that we can hear you talk. We are often invisible to your human eyes, and we can hear and see you. It is necessary, in order to communicate with you, that we should be able to speak your language. So, to meet the necessity, we learn your language. It is easy for us for we have what you would call phenomenal memories. We never forget anything that we wish to remember.

You people of earth can learn to do all of these things for already some of you can do them. But the one great and important thing that we want you to do is to learn to send out impersonal Divine love. On the planets near the Earth we do that and it has become second nature to us. Instead of using force to accomplish our desires we send out love, which is the greatest power in the universe. When we desire to build a city, for instance, all those engaged in the project, before they begin, send thoughts of pure love to one another and keep those thoughts sustained throughout the whole time of planning and construction. This causes everything to move so smoothly that it seems as if the city almost builds itself.

If there is disagreement it is settled by quiet, reasonable discussion and soon the best plan is followed. This is only an example of the power of love. In quarreling and trying to force your opponents to adopt your way, confusion exists and much time and effort is taken to accomplish that which should be easily done.

Life is Love, Love is Life, and Life and God are one and the same. Life is everywhere, in everything, for it is existence. In the depths of creation Love reigns supreme, though on the surface it may seem to be lacking. The reader may think that we have left the subject of space ships, but this is still on the subject. That is the way our space ships are built—with love. The ideas for the invention of these very successful "birds of the air," as we lovingly call them, all came to us in love, never in bickering or dislike of any one. All great inventors have loved their inventions and those for whom the inventions were made.

Love is the explanation of our visits to the planet Earth. That is the only reason for our coming. We can see the terrible turmoil and confusion on the Earth caused by man's mistaken idea that force rules and overcomes all that is wrong. This is far from the truth, for force itself is entirely wrong. Nothing lasting has ever been accomplished by force. We have learned that by thinking and reasoning, for we are reasonable beings. Man is supposed to be a reasonable being but the fact is that he is not. He is governed by his emotions almost entirely. Emotions cause prejudice and prejudices cause emotions. Of course there are good emotions, and love is one of these and the most powerful. But in order to be powerful it must be pure, Divine love, not the possessive emotion that is sometimes, in fact often, called love.

The love that I am speaking of is entirely unselfish. It is the pure Love of God which will flow through any human heart if it is open and unobstructed by wrong mental images. You may not think that we are human, but we are very like you, we have minds to think and hearts to love, and we use them to good purpose.

You have minds and hearts but it seems to us who watch you that you do not use either. You must learn to use both mind and heart if you wish to untangle the mess that you are in. We love you as we love every living being, and again I say we are ready to help you in any way we can. The first way would probably be to teach you to build really good space ships. Yours are noisy and they polute the air with harmful smokes and gases. We fly without noise or smoke. After you have built some like ours you will be able easily to visit our planets as well as the moon. But not for purposes of war, but as friendly visitors desiring to understand the lives of their neighbors. The time is past when the little earth was seemingly a large globe, and travel from one place to another was on foot or horseback or in horse drawn vehicles. Now distances are short on the surface of the Earth and also short between the Earth and other planets. Perhaps I have repeated this too often, but I hope to make it sink into the minds and hearts of those who read. Then they will spread the truth among their friends and acquaintances with good results. Education is what is needed at this time.

Education is the purpose of this book. There is not much to say but what is said is right to the point and means a great deal. After this assurance of our friendship you who dwell on the Earth will have no fear when we visit your planet, and since we speak your language fluently we will be able to plan together how to educate the mass of people on Earth so that they may desire peaceful living without conflict of any kind, either physical or mental.

This book is easy to read and is only an opening wedge, so to speak. It is a forerunner of more erudite ones to follow. Those which follow will be books of science and will be concerned with the building and operating of space craft. The dictation of these will be from scientists to scientists.

With these words I bid you farewell. My love and blessing is with you in all your endeavors. My name would mean nothing to you, but those who are sensitive will feel my love and blessing.

From Planet Pluto With Brotherly Love

The inhabitants of the Planet Pluto are very similar to those of the Earth. Our bodies are like yours in every respect. Our height is like yours, being different with each individual. Some tall, some short, some medium in height. Indeed, I think the Planet Pluto resembles the Earth more closely than any of the other planets, except in one important respect—we live in peace and brotherly love.

There are no wars, no quarrels, no crimes, such as robbery, murder etc. The Earth is the only planet in this solar system which is not peaceful and happy. This seems very strange, and surely something could be done to eliminate this condition and bring peace and happiness to the Earth.

There are many loving Earth people now, who are devoting themselves to works of charity. There are many organizations active in helping the needy and the sick. There are free schools and colleges for the education of the youth of the land. When we see all this which is beautiful, we wonder how there can be the ruthless competition in business, and the wars which are always being waged on some part of the Earth.

Has there ever been a time when peace prevailed over the entire surface of the globe? There has never been such a time.

Why? We who are looking on ask, why? It is said that there is always a reason for everything, so there must be a reason for this sad state of affairs. We must look and see if we can find the cause.

In what way does the Earth differ from the other planets, which never have wars? The cause may perhaps be found in the number of nationalities, which are different in language and appearance. One nation cannot understand the language of another without study in school. Customs and habits of everyday life also differ.

In early times there were continual

wars between peoples of different countries for the purpose of carrying away spoil. The soldiers returned from the war laden with riches taken from the enemy, and driving before them slaves which were made from the captives of war.

There was usually no good reason for the war. One country accused the other of stepping over the boundary line, perhaps. But usually there was only the difference in language and the desire for spoil.

At one time the Roman Empire owned most of the Earth. At another time Spain became most powerful. The tiny country of England once bragged that "the sun never sets on British possessions."

At this very moment wars are being fought and young men are being drafted into the army—taken from their homes to fight for they know not what.

This has been the history of the Planet Earth. A sad history it has been. A record of bloodshed and robbery. We shall try to find the reason for this and try to find a remedy.

The reason seems to be a strong feeling of separation between nations and a strong desire for the acquiring of riches by any means. When we look closer we see that the riches were enjoyed by a very small number of the population—by those in power as rulers and their associates. The great majority of the people received little benefit.

What was lacking on the Earth that we of the other planets possessed? The lacking quality was love for God. With love for God, the Father of all, love for man would follow.

In very early times the Israelites considered themselves the chosen people of God. All others were aliens. But these people did not love their God as a Heavenly Father, they feared Him as a mighty King. They were the chosen people of this mighty King and all others were their enemies. There was no love in their religion. In the Old Testament it is stated, "The Lord Thy God is a jealous God." Never was He a loving Father.

This was changed with the advent of Jesus, the Christ, whose teaching was love. Love for God the Father and love for their brother men was the teaching preached and emphasized. His disciples lived and preached this teaching and they had many followers. But, alas, as time moved on, there were differences of opinion among his followers, arguments over trivial matters of ritual. Instead of one church there were many, and one which gained power would persecute the others.

So the beautiful teaching of love for God and for all humanity received only lip service, it did not penetrate into the hearts of the majority. There were saints who lived the teaching but they were a very small minority. War and bloodshed did not cease, only the cause was different. One religion would be in power and all others must be crushed. Where was the beautiful teaching of love for God and man?

Once more the rich in worldly goods were in power, acting under the pretense of religion. You see, we on Pluto have watched the Earth, for we have been able to see that which was taking place just as easily as one country could follow events in another. More easily than the primitive countries with their lack of transportation could.

We of Pluto can read minds, as some of mankind can do, but with us it is universal. In the minds of the people of Earth we saw the reason for their greed and cruelty. Their thoughts were almost always busy with self. The mothers of families were the only ones with unselfish love for others, they would sacrifice their own comfort for the welfare of their little ones. We looked into the minds of the fathers and found that many of them also loved their children devotedly and some husbands and wives truly loved each other unselfishly.

But beyond this love did not go. There was no love for the neighbors or for God Almighty. There was suspicion for the neighbors and fear for God. How different it was on Pluto. Our love flowed forth to all those around us, and rose to our Heavenly Father with devotion and joy.

With true love comes joy and peace. When a whole population loves they live in joy and peace. There cannot be war and destruction. There cannot be cheating and trickery. Now we have found the cause of all the unhappiness on Earth, it is caused by lack of love for God and their brother man. What about the religions of Earth, is there not love in them? Yes, in the religions love can be found, but there is much fear mixed with love for God, and love for each other does not go beyond those who practice the same religion, the same ceremonies, and the same dogmas. There have been terrible wars waged in the name of religion. Much cruelty—even torture—has been practiced in the name of religion, even in the same nation.

The Crusades of the middle ages were wars waged by the Christians against the Moslems in the name of Christ Jesus. Love was forgotten and cruelty reigned supreme. This is only one example of how the followers of a religion which taught love, completely ignored that teaching.

If it were understood and realized that there is one Source of all life, one Source only, then humanity would be brought together in peace and love. If the Source were loved and worshipped by all, and it were understood that all life proceeded from that source, then the realization of brotherhood would follow. We of Pluto have understood this and felt and practiced this love for many centuries, more than we can count. We do not remember a time when we did not love and worship the One Great Source of all life. We realize that we all have come forth from the One Great Source of Life and we know in our minds and hearts that we all are the One in expression. All are the One Life in manifestation.

Then how could one of us hurt another? How could there be wars, greed and hatred? These could not be for we know — really know — that we are all One, being parts of the One Great Life from which all that is comes forth. All the planets know this except the planet Earth. Why is this so? Why do not the people of Earth know in the depths of their beings that all are one—all children of the One Great Father? Why do they not know that when they injure their brother they are injuring themselves, for all life is One Life, there is no separation.

The Earth has never been without great teachers who have preached and prophesied, urging their hearers to worship their God and love one another. They had followers who listened to their words, but very few took their teaching into their hearts and lived it. But I am thankful that I can say that at the present time there is a glimmer of hope that this denseness will be penetrated by the Light which never fails.

In many parts of the Earth people have come together in groups and listen to the words of illumined ones who live and understand. Many of these groups have been formed in the United States of America. They all teach love and unity. The Light is spreading in all directions and hearts are filling with love. But still there are wars raging upon the Earth. It seems that war has become a habit, the only way that is known to settle a dispute. How stupid this is! Yes, stupid is the only word for it. How strange that people who are otherwise intelligent should still cling to the practice of war, with all the misery and suffering that it causes.

You who read these words can help to do away with war. How can an indivdual in private life do anything to prevent war? By prayer to God Almighty, and He is not far off in the sky but within you, and within all that lives. For God and Life are the same. "The prayer of a righteous man availeth much," So no one is helpless, anyone can pray with a heart full of love for God and humanity. Pray more than twice a day. At any time, in any place, your thought can fly forth carrying love and supplication, with faith that the prayer shall be answered. Some groups use decrees, which are very good. There is no hard and fast rule for communicating with the Father within. Desire and love with faith are all that is needed.

If the desire for peace on earth is strong, a habit is soon formed to send out prayers or decrees very frequently without pausing in whatever you may be doing. The hands may be busy but thought is free to rise to any height. "Peace on Earth, goodwill toward men" the angels sang when Jesus the Christ was born. We on the planet Pluto heard the wonderful chorus and know that this is true.

There is much skepticism on the planet Earth. It is thought by many that much of the beautiful teaching in the Bible is false, only stories or parables to express spiritual teaching. True, there are parables given as such, but the so-called miracles were true and the same could be performed now if mankind had faith and enough love. "Ask and it shall be given unto you." But there must be no doubt in the asking. Asking with doubt in the mind is no better than not asking at all. Also when decrees are given they must be given with faith that that which they demand is an accomplished fact. They must be given with love and faith in God and love and faith in man.

This is being taught by many organizations on the Earth today and many hundreds of people are practicing this. It is a practice for individuals in their homes at any time of the day or night. Calamities have been averted by this means. Great earthquakes, tidal waves, storms of thunder and lightning have been controlled and either eliminated or made very much less severe. Predictions have failed to come to pass and many persons have believed that the prophets were mistaken. Only those who have been sending forth the prayers and decrees have known why the predicted calamity did not come as had been predicted.

Wonderful is the love of God for man.

Every opportunity is given humanity to reform, change their ways of greed and battle, for ways of love and peace. We other planets were inspired by God to offer our assistace and to tell of our own ways of living in peace and love. We are all very happy to do anything we can to help. By means of these little booklets we introduce ourselves and offer our friendship.

There has always been friendship and free communication between all the planets in this solar system with the exception of the planet Earth. The inhabitants of that planet have held aloof. Many years ago it was believed that the Earth was flat and if one travelled too far he would fall off the edge. In the mind of man the Earth was all. There was no other life.

Now, by means of powerful instruments and life-long study by those called astronomers, the fact has been discovered that the Earth and all other planets are globes, not flat surfaces. From the Earth astronauts are now being sent up in especially constructed ships—we would call them—to explore the spheres around the Earth. We are watching with interest and if they should land we would greet them cordially.

It is very possible that the astronauts may be able to land on one of the planets or on the moon. They are learning much about travel in the higher realms above the planet Earth. If they do land they will find much to interest them. The large population, the towns and cities, the trees and flowers, all so much like the Earth. We can read minds and we can speak any language, so there will be no obstacle in the way of communication. How happy we shall be if one day we see them land.

Our little children will run forth to greet them, for the little ones are much interested in what they have been told about life and living, and their minds and hearts are open and receptive to new experiences. They know that there is one God, Creator of all that is; they know that God is Love and they are afraid of nothing. They are like the little children of Earth in their innocence and activity.

It is the same on all the planets. No matter where the astronauts may land they will be cordially greeted.

Everywhere is life and life and God are One, the only One that is. We know that we are all brothers, children of the one Father. Our lives are lived in love and peace for we truly know in the depths of our beings that all life is one life, there is no separation.

This is being taught now in many places on the planet Earth. When we come close to the Earth we can hear what is being said. Walls do not shut us out, we can pass through them with ease. We do not go with idle curiosity but with love and a desire to be of help.

We are pleased to hear the true teaching being given in many groups. By far the greatest number of them are in the United States of America. Next in number are the other English speaking peoples.

The knowledge that life and God are one and that all is God, there is no separation, is doing much to bring peace and love among nations. In God we live and move and have our being, and by God we live and move and have our being. For there is only one that acts and that is God. It is difficult to understand this at first for we feel as if we were the actors. That is because the connection is so close between God and us. In fact there is no division, all is one and that One is God.

That might make it seem that we do not exist. We do exist in the mind and heart of the Creator for Creator and created are One substance and that substance is the only substance everywhere. Pure substance fills all seeming space and from it all is formed. There are no empty spaces anywhere. The human eye cannot see the shining substance, just as the human ear cannot hear the music of the planets moving in their orbits. There is a musical sound from everything that moves, and all is moving in the one shining substance that is everywhere. Highly illumined ones see and feel and hear, but the vast majority of mankind are oblivious to the beauty in which they live.

We of the planet Pluto learned the truth of life many eons ago and we have never forgotten. The joy of living in this realization is very great, and it is our strong desire that our brothers of the Earth shall attain this realization and live in this joy. Our prayers go out to the One Great Source of all being, in whom all is, was, and ever shall be. It may seem that prayers should not be needed since all is one. In life there are many seeming contradictions, which are really not contradictions to a loving heart and a clear mind. All creation is governed by law—Divine law. These laws originate in the Source of all being. There is a law that the created shall love and worship the Creator. The Creator does love His creation. When the created ones do their part in loving and worshiping the Creator all is truly one and that One is God.

So prayers are needed from all creation. The birds and animals unconsciously send forth love in their feelings of joy and life. They live their lives by instinct, they do not reason, they feel and act as they are moved to act. The higher forms of creation have been given the power to think and reason. On the planet Earth this power has been neglected, and instead of pure reason the emotions of liking and disliking have been lived by to a great extent. This has been the cause of many wars. If the rulers of the nations would come together and discuss their problems with reason and love for each other instead of unreasonable dislike, many wars would be prevented.

This would not be difficult. Man has caused all his troubles and agony by lack of love. In the private lives of the people only their own family and some friends are loved. This is not the way to live. There should be love for all the population whether seen or unseen, whether congenial or not.

This is the way of life on Pluto. It has always been the way of life and we are very happy people. All differences of opinion are discussed with reason. Each is carefully considered and finally the most reasonable action is pursued. This is not difficult to do because there is no egotism, no selfishness, love reigns supreme.

That is the way our planet is ruled, entirely by reason, and I should add, by love. Hatred is unknown. Dear people of Earth you could do this, for you are not on the whole stupid or lacking in intelligence. Those in important positions are intelligent, but many are lacking in pure love for all creation. Only their own country is loved, other countries are beyond the pale, as it were.

For happy peaceful living there must be love for all, not for a selected few. How cold and lifeless this seems, although love for a few is better than no love at all. There are individuals who love no one but themselves and the feeling for themselves is not love but greed.

But in the darkness there is a glimmer of light. Many groups have been formed on the Earth for the purpose of studying the truth of living, and these are sending out much love and light to all humanity. They are devoted people, devoted to the service of God and humanity. They unselfishly give much time to sending forth love, and love and light are one.

This is not done yet in all the countries of the Earth, but it is spreading among the English speaking people, and like a great fire it will eventually spread into all civilized countries, and from there what should stop it?

When we of Pluto discovered these beautiful groups, with their earnestness and high understanding, our hearts thrilled with joy and our love poured out to mingle with theirs. So this message from Pluto ends on a note of strong encouragement. Our love goes out to you of the planet Earth, and we hope that the time will come when we may visit you and you may visit us, and instead of writing we may converse together.

So we bid you farewell until that happy day.

Deepspace 85-foot diameter tracking antenna, Woomera, Australia.

NASA

Neptune From Experience Gives Advice

This is the seventh writing from the planets of the solar system of which the planet Earth is a part. It is Neptune speaking.

This writing is following close after that of Saturn, for the planets in conference had agreed that Saturn should inform mankind of the very serious situation on the Earth and close around it. Beloved Saturn accepted that unpleasant duty and performed it well. He exposed the machinations of certain beings in human form called Watchers or Money Changers. He also spoke of the dark forces hovering close to the Earth and even descending onto the Earth, and certain ones entering into the inner consciousness of individuals who were open to them because of selfishness, greed and lack of love for God, the source of all life.

Saturn performed his task, and I was called on to follow close after him because the planet Neptune had been attacked by these dark forces and had conquered and driven them away. They fled before the light that we poured forth and have never dared to return. Darkness disappears in the Light of God.

It is my duty to tell you about the experience of the population of Neptune so that the people of Earth can follow our example as quickly as possible, for the longer these dark forces are ignored the stronger they become, drawing to them others like unto themselves.

It was many years ago that the beautiful planet Neptune became a prey of these hideous forces. With us, also, they were preceded by the beings which seemed to be physical beings like ourselves. Apparently prosperous business men, the same as many others. As Saturn said, they were like vampire bats sucking the blood of the planet.

When we came close to the Earth and saw these manipulators of the money system and saw behind them the black pall decending very close to the Earth, we knew from experience what it was and we planned to inform the Earth of our experience. We were in a very serious condition, but thanks be to God, we got completely rid of the Watchers and their following dark forces.

You of the Earth can do likewise when you understand what is taking place on and around your planet. So this writing will be devoted entirely to telling of our experience. We would like to tell you about our present life on our beautiful planet, but I cannot enter into that, for the most important thing is to give you the information that will help you get rid of these vampires and their following dark forces.

First it was necessary to tell you that this situation existed, and Saturn has done that. Next I will give you an account of how we of Neptune cleared our atmosphere of the darkness after getting rid of the fiends who posed as our brothers.

To look at them they appeared to be no different from any of our prosperous business men, but they were dominated by greed and were without scruple in the method of obtaining wealth. Their hearts were utterly without love. There was no feeling of sympathy for those in need, all their thought was on themselves and the amassing of riches. When we look at the Earth we see similar ones very active. These are all in private life, they hold no official positions. Your government does not know who they are or what they are.

It was the same with us, it was a long time before we knew them for what they were, and after we did know them we had to find a plan to get rid of them. You of the Earth are in the same position. Some of your people now have discovered these prosperous men and know what they are, but the majority of the population knows nothing of them and if they hear about them believe it is a ridiculous mistake.

We of Neptune see them clearly and assure you that what you have been told is truth. When we discovered them and knew them for what they were, we called meetings of all our governmental bodies to discuss the way to get rid of them. We knew that they were entirely evil and so could be conquered by the opposite, which is good. They loved the darkness and so could be driven away by the light. When the sun rises all is light. So it was planned that many groups would be formed all over the planet, for the purpose of calling forth much light which would be directed onto these beings.

On your Earth there are now many groups of all sizes which are active in studying Truth and practicing it. So no groups would have to be called together, those that are already formed could take up the work. They could meet for the especial purpose of praying, decreeing, calling on God for help to expel the dark forces. These forces fear the light, the Light of God which never fails.

So the only thing that we can say is to have more meetings, pray more often, decree in private, at home many times a day. The darkness around your planet is very thick and much light will be needed to break through it and drive it away.

Each one of you examine yourselves to be sure there is no feeling of selfishness or greed within your mind or heart, not even the smallest indication of it. Pure unselfish love is light from which the dark forces flee. They cannot enter any mind or heart which is full of pure, unselfish love.

This is what we did on the Planet Neptune. It took effect and the dark forces disappeared. Then we turned our attention on the seeming business men who were getting the finances of the planet into very bad shape. They were profiting by the losses of others. Poverty was the lot of the majority while the few lived in wealth and more than plenty.

This has been the condition on Earth for many centuries. There has been poverty for the majority, wealth for a very few. It had been accepted as the natural way of life. There were kind hearted people who gave alms to those in need; groups of women met to sew and make garments for the poor. Parties were given at which a price was charged and the money used to help the indigent.

In earlier times there were beggars on the street corners holding cups in which the passers-by dropped small coins. It was accepted by all to be the natural way of life.

On Neptune it had not been the natural way of life. There had been sufficient for all. Poverty was unknown and so also was extreme wealth. The people were all occupied in various ways. There were farmers, merchants, sellers of produce. There were dress makers, tailors, fishers, etc. Every need was supplied by honest exchange of products or work.

There were writers of books; there were musicians, artists, both painters and sculptors; every occupation that was needed, there was. The planet was a happy place until the Watchers and Money Changers arrived.

They posed as business men and looked the part. But in reality they were aliens, we know not where from. It is the same at present on your planet Earth. These aliens found their way onto the Earth and made it their home. They resemble the original population in looks and actions, but in thought and feeling they are far different.

After we cleared the atmosphere of the dark forces we turned our attention to these flesh and blood demons. It was more difficult to get rid of them because they seemed to be an integrate part of the community. How could we distinguish them from other business men?

In looks they were the same, but in actions they were different. For one thing they were very pompous, very conceited and haughty. They looked down on plain people as if they were of no account. If they were watched awhile it was seen that they completely lacked sympathy with anyone who needed help or encouragement.

If you, our brothers of the Earth look carefully you will see the same thing. They are not normal persons. The mark of the beast is on them. If you will single them out and put your attention on them you will be sure to catch them in some act of dishonesty.

It requires attention, unremitting attention. It will have to be done by those who are associated with them in some way. Not necessarily in a business way but in any association in daily living. Employer and servant; acquaintances in society; associates in business; they may be any one of these.

There is one trait among them all, they are all conceited and pompous, looking down on all they associate with. If they are carefully watched they will be caught in some unlawful act for which they can be prosecuted.

So it was on Neptune, and when we discovered the transgressors they were prosecuted, convicted, and thrown into prison, where they spent the rest of their lives. Short sentences would be of no avail, it must be for life.

It was not easy but it was done, and what we have done you of Earth can do. Do not slacken for a moment in your attention. They are wiley and full of tricks, but we conquered them, and their children fled from the planet into the far distance.

The planet Neptune is now carefree and is a place of beauty and peace. It is our strong desire that our brothers and sisters of the planet Earth shall heed the warning of Saturn, and follow our example in getting completely free of the demons and the dark forces which follow them.

Our planet is now very beautiful and we are living in peace and love. There is never conflict of any kind, all is harmony and joy.

Uranus Lover of Man Speaks

The name of this planet is Uranus. It is a large planet and much power flows from it into the atmosphere surrounding it. I who am sending this message am also called Uranus. The accent in this name is on the first syllable.

She who is taking this message felt my presence years ago and it was an experience she never forgot. One day she was walking from one room to another in her house and as she opened the door a tremendous power of joy and love flowed through her being. It was so strong that she felt she might fall to the floor. She seized the door-knob and leaned against the door.

This joy and love remained strong within her for months, then gradually became less but it has never entirely left her.

I am giving this as an example of the power which I give forth in love and joy. My action is sudden and my love is strong. This is also the disposition of my people, those who inhabit this planet.

There is no fear or hesitation on the planet Uranus. Where love and joy are present there can be no fear or hesitation.

Dear ones of Earth, we of Uranus love you and our desire is to help you to understand the meaning of Life, the joy of peace and love, the worship of the Great Life which fills all that is, making all One.

The cruelty and greed that we see on the Earth makes our hearts ache and dims our joy. Life can be so beautiful and could be so on the Earth if man could only be made to understand that Love is the great power, not force.

Almost all of the history of the Earth has been accounts of battles and bloodshed. One country fighting another in order to despoil it. In early times enslaving the people and using them to labor in the mines and fields under the whips of overseers. Now is the age of invention so machines are used to do the work, but there is still war and bloodshed on the Earth.

We see all this from our planet and our great desire is to see joy and love take its place. We join the other planets of this solar system in inviting mankind to visit us and experience the joy and peace of our lives.

Our flying saucers as you call them have not flown over the Earth with evil intent but only with the desire to make friends with you, our brothers. In the first booklet of the series the building of space ships was urged and all the planets strongly advise this. We shall only mention this for it has been well covered in the first booklet.

We of Uranus would be pleased to have you come to our planet as our guests. I will tell you what kind of beings we are. We are of flesh, blood, bone etc., just as you are. We are not very tall, as are the people of Venus, nor are we very short. We vary somewhat in height which is usually medium. We are strong and healthy, sickness is unknown, for no one who is loving and full of joy can be sick.

Just try it yourselves and see. If you stop worrying, stop complaining, stop fighting and struggling you will never be sick. Love and joy are better than any medicine. We have heard of sickness but none of us have ever experienced it.

Another thing—we are careful not to overeat and we do not drink spirituous liquors. Being well and healthy we do not feel the need of any stimulant; tobacco, alcohol or drugs of any kind. Our sensible way of living makes us healthy and our good health makes life joyful and radiant.

Come and see us on our planet and you will understand that which I am telling you. Eons ago we were not like this. We forgot the Great Source of life, and worry and struggle took possession of us. We were then very much as you are now. But a great Teacher arose in our midst. He spoke eloquently and with conviction and persuasion.

Some of us listened to him and followed in his steps. Others saw the benefit of this teaching and believed and practiced it. It was the teaching of love for each other and oneness with the Great Source of Life. It was the same teaching that you people of Earth received centuries ago from the beloved One called Jesus the Christ. You loved your Teacher but you misunderstood much of his teaching, and what you did understand you did not practice. Terrible cruelties were practiced by men on others who did not believe exactly as they did; on those whose ceremonies were different. The great central teaching of love for God and mankind was neglected and importance was given to insignificant little differences in ritual.

Dear ones of Earth, many of you now have had your eyes — of the Spirit — opened and the true teaching of your beloved Master is understood and even practiced. Love—brotherly love—is coming forth into the world of humanity. In the midst of wars, chicanery, and greed a spark of light is glowing.

It is called the New Age Teaching and it is the true teaching of Jesus the Christ, unadulterated and pure. Many groups on the Earth are studying and practicing this which is the truth.

We from the planet Uranus see this when we come close to the Earth, watch and listen with love and rejoicing, and give our blessings and best wishes to the teachers and students of this true religion. Although the Earth is in a turmoil of battles and catastrophes, cruelty and misery, the little spark is growing, and is destined to spread over the whole Earth.

We of the planet Uranus will rejoice with you of Earth when this time comes.

It has been decided to give in this paper a very brief and simple explanation of astrology. In ancient times astrology was a very deep study and was practiced by many who were prophets of coming events. The rulers of great and powerful nations had an astrologer always in their entourage and at their beck and call.

In modern times many private individuals have dabbled in astrology in a very superficial way, almost as a pastime, one might say. This writing will necessarily be brief but it will be accurate and true. Astrology is the study of the effect of the stars upon the planet Earth and its inhabitants. First of all we must admit that the stars do have an effect on the Earth and therefore all living beings on Earth feel the effect. But, as all good teachers explain, humanity does not have to be a slave to these effects.

When the signs of the zodiac are studied in connection with the birth date of an individual, that individual can take the predicted events as a possibility but not inevitable. He is endowed with freedom of choice and he may call on the God within him to guide him into a better path.

No man, woman or child is helpless because of what the stars show in his horoscope. The stars warn but cannot compel. What are the stars? They can be seen shining in the sky especially when the atmosphere is clear and dry, as in the mountains or on the desert.

The sun is a star but it is not thought of in that way on Earth, it is the planets, shining with reflected light that are thought of and spoken of on Earth as stars.

That is the reason for this discourse. Uranus is one of the stars that influences the people of Earth. Venus, Jupiter, Saturn, Mercury are others. There is a magnetic current flowing from all of these bodies and it is felt by the living beings on each.

Every planet exerts a pull on others in its radius. The Earth affects those near it just as they affect the Earth. This was not understood by ancient astrologers but your modern astronomers know it. This pull is felt not only by the planet itself but by all that lives upon the planet. It can be of benefit or it can be detrimental to the living body.

Astrology was studied by wise men of old to foretell the futures of human beings, especially of kings and rulers. Usually a king of a country, among his courtiers had an astrologer who advised him according to what the stars showed in his horoscope. The day, month and year of birth of the ruler and the position of the planets at the time the horoscope was cast were studied by the astrologer, who drew up a chart and judged by that whether the time was propitious or not for entering into war or keeping the country in peace.

The prognostcations were not always correct, and many an astrologer was executed by the command of an angry ruler, who had relied on his advice to enter into war only to be defeated.

At the present time astrology is studied and practiced by private individuals who believe they can guide their daily actions by this knowledge.

It is a weak reed on which to lean, but in one way it can be used to advantage, and that is in the study of character. The stars that were in the sky at the time of birth do have an effect on the character and propensities of the subject. However, they do not compel the action of the one born under their rays. The man or woman whose strong desire is to lead a good life, by making an effort and having faith in prayer to God can ignore the horoscope.

Some may say, "Then why bother with astrology at all?" This is a sensible question. The reason is that by knowing what the influences of the stars are in an individuals life, he is forewarned and will not allow himself to be guided by his emotions, but by careful consideration of the facts of a situation.

So now we shall briefly consider the effect of the various planets on the planet Earth.

There are eight well known planets and from time to time the astronomers of Earth discover another which shows in their telescopes. These newer ones are not so close to the Earth and therefore have little effect on this planet.

The planet Mars is near the Earth and the modern astronauts are eager to reach it and land upon it. It is not a large planet but the vibrations from it have an effect on the planet Earth.

For certain reasons the ancient astrologers were neglectful of this planet and confined their work to the larger planets in the solar system of which the earth is a part. Very important ones were Jupiter and Saturn.

They both have a very strong effect on the planet Earth and therefore on the lives of the inhabitants of Earth. As shown in the horoscopes drawn up by the astrologers, Jupiter was a planet which brought happiness and good fortune, while Saturn had an opposite influence. The word saturnine in your language was derived from the name of the planet Saturn.

The rotation of the Earth and its movement around the sun bring it close to the other planets or far from them. So it comes under the influence of one planet or another depending on the position of the Earth itself. The Earth and the other planets being spherical in shape this brings about a great variety of conjunctions, or close approaches of planets to each other.

The nearness of the planets is very important, for the strong vibrations that flow forth from each planet meet and mingle bringing changes in the atmosphere and in the soil underfoot. The inhabitants of the planets feel this and it has an influence on their physical bodies, causing different emotions in the spiritual bodies.

So the study of astrology and also of astronomy is a study of the movements of the planets as they journey around the sun. In the study of astronomy there is no attention paid to the effect this has on the human being. The study of astrology deals entirely with that phase.

In drawing up a horoscope attention is paid to the exact location on Earth where the subject of the inquiry was born. This is very important for the turning of the Earth will bring that spot into conjunction with a certain planet at a certain time. So the exact time of birth is also very important. All this has an effect upon the infant as it comes into the world and strongly influences the personality. In ancient times it was believed that this influence was too strong to be broken, but it has been found by the study of many subjects that this is not true, the spiritual being of man can triumph over any prognostication in a horoscope; and the spiritual being of man can reign supreme over any misfortune.

Man is spirit, not the body of flesh. The flesh body is the container only. The soul is spirit and lives forever, the physical body decays and is no more. It is very difficult for mankind to get the feeling of this. The physical body is so full of sensations, pains, aches, and thrills of joy. All actions in the outer world of living are seemingly performed by the physical body. From the time of birth the little baby feels the sensations of the physical body and so it continues until the end of physical life.

But the real being is the soul which lives the inner life, and the inner life is the life of spirit not the life of matter. Spirit is everywhere, it is not confined to one locality. It cannot be held to one place, it goes out in thought everywhere.

This has been taught by the philosophers for ages, but man has largely ignored the teaching and has thought of himself as a physical body living the outer life. "As a man thinketh in his heart so is he."

Notice that the word "heart" is used in this well known saying, not "mind." The heart is deep within; the mind is near the surface. The heart spoken of is not the physical organ; it is the spirit.

What has this to do with astrology? It has much to do with it, but it has largely been ignored. The effect of the planets on the physical being has been studied and recorded; the spirit has been entirely overlooked. The spirit is free and cannot be bound by rules and regulations, nor can it be a slave to the vibrations coming from the planets.

Herein is the power vested in humanity. As God is, so is humanity. God is all, all that is, including humanity. This is not blasphemy, it is truth. "In Him we live and move and have our being." The spirit which is man, lives and moves in the One Spirit which is called God. This Great Spirit is everywhere—It is all. In It, by It and for It the human being lives, one with all Spirit, one with God, who is Spirit.

How can the physical effect of any planet near the Earth control the spirit of Man, which is one with the Spirit of God? It is only when the spirit of man allows the physical to take control that this can be. When this is understood astrology can be a help to the individual. It will show what tendencies of character to guard against, and forewarn concerning events which may take place and could be guarded against.

It is not for recreation or to be carelessly dabbled in. If studied at all it should be studied seriously. Too many persons merely play with it. Nothing that affects the spirit of man should be played with lightly, and astrology affects the spirit as well as the physical body. If one desires to make a real study of astrology he can find a teacher without much difficulty; or if he simply wishes to know how the stars affect his own life he can find a genuine astrologer who will cast his horoscope for him, of course making a charge for the work.

The planet of which I am the Ruler, Uranus, is a large planet and its effect on the Earth and mankind is very strong. With her permission I shall give as an example the experience of the one who is writing these words at my dictation.

Some years ago she was attending lectures given by a soul advanced in the new teaching. He again and again urged his hearers to give up the self and allow the Christ within to guide the life. She felt that she should do this, but hesitated because of fear that demands would be made on her that would be very difficult and unpleasant. She was thinking of this one day when the words came into her mind, "But think how much you will gain."

This gave her courage and she decided to give herself up to God. So she prayed to God, saying, "Father, God, I give myself up to Thee, though I am only giving that which is Thine already." There was no answer and she had not expected an answer, but a few days later she had the experience which was recounted at the beginning of this writing.

I, Uranus, poured my strong vibration into her and it was a shock at the time, but the effect that was left in her was joy and love. She has always been grateful for that experience.

Strong and sudden action is characteristic of Uranus. Strong and sudden but never harmful, always beneficial for it comes in love. The planet Uranus, through me its leader, pours forth love and joy which flows through it from the Source of all creation, God.

God is all and all is God. There is no other anywhere. Life is all and all is Life. Life and God are synonymous words.

Now to go back to astrology. Astrology, seriously studied, can be an aid in living a good life. Astrology as a pastime can be dangerous. It is much better to give your heart and mind into the keeping of God, the Father of all, praying for His help and guidance. With these words Uranus bids the people of Earth farewell.

Saturn
Planet of Peace
Sends Warning

This is the sixth paper from the planets in this solar system and it is from the Planet Saturn, spoken by the Ruler of that planet whose name is Saturn. It is coming to the people of Earth through the same human channel or instrument, as it is called. She has had much experience in receiving and writing from dictation from distant spheres. This is called telepathy. Now, after this introduction, we shall proceed with the writing of the sixth booklet.

There is a great desire among the planets near the Earth—and this is also felt by the Great White Brotherhood of the planes above the Earth—that mankind may learn to live in peace and love as the inhabitants of the other planets live.

It has been thought that if the inhabitants of the Earth were informed concerning the happy lives of the inhabitants of the other planets, it might inspire them to make an effort to achieve this peace and joy for themselves.

Now, after that rather lengthy introduction we shall confine ourselves to the planet Saturn. The people of Saturn are serious and much in earnest about everything they do, there is no foolishness or frivolity in their natures. This does not mean that they are gloomy or sad. No indeed, they are cheerful and happy, but not frivolous. They do not waste anything but make good use of everything they have.

They, like all the other planets except the planet Earth, live as the Great Teacher of Nazareth urged the people of Earth to live, in brotherly love. There is no greedy competition in business; there are no wars; there is no cheating; there is no selfishness of any kind. They live the life that the religious teachers, priests and ministers, preach and pray for.

It is the life of pure love, the only life of true joy and happiness. It is worth a kingdom to learn this and earn this. For it must be earned by most individuals, only a few come into the world perfect, without temptation. To strive after perfection is the first step and perseverance is the second. Never to criticize others but know that all have their temptations, and above all to know that within each one is the Spirit of Life or God, different names for the same Reality. This is the philosophy—or you may call it religion—of the inhabitants of the planet Saturn. From early childhood we are instructed in this philosophy by our parents and they set us an example by living that which they teach.

The inhabitants of Saturn are not different looking than the prevailing race of the Earth, though there is a shining light in our eyes that is seldom seen in the eyes of mankind. It is the light of the God-presence shining out. You will see it in the eyes of some of the people of Earth but on Saturn it is in all without exception.

This is because we constantly feel the presence of God within us. This consciousness causes us to live together in perfect love and accord. Dear Ones of Earth, you can reach this same state of love and peace if you cultivate the constant feeling and belief in the presence of God within you.

I hear a question, has Saturn always been like that? Yes, we have always been like that and we daily give thanks for this knowledge. We have never asked for lives of free will, we have lived always according to the will of our Father God. Thus we have been saved from many mistakes and much unhappiness.

We firmly believe that the people of Earth are destined to attain this way of life and we urge you not to hesitate, but to give yourselves into the care and direction of your God.

Now, what about the daily lives of our people? How do we live? Have we a government and officials to manage the government? Have we laws and the enforcement of laws?

These questions shall be answered. Yes, we have a government and officials to manage it. All would be confusion without that. We have a government and officials and one supreme ruler. But here the likeness to your governments ceases. There is no necessity for law enforcement. Now this will seem very strange to you but it is true. Without any exception all those on this planet are law-abiding citizens. Certain rules and regulations have been decided upon in conference by the officials, and these rules are followed by every citizen without exception.

There is no poverty so there is no temptation to steal. The love of God is in every heart and this leads to love of each other. We are living the life that the Angels above the Earth sang of on Christmas Day.

You see we are well acquainted with your planet and its people. We hope that you will also become well acquainted with us and our planet. Without conceit we can say that a visit to Saturn would open your hearts and minds to much that you have never experienced on your Earth. It is our strong desire that you should visit us and see and experience for yourselves our way of living. We could come for you in our space ships, for they are real and solid. They are not ephemeral visions. We also have the hope that after you have visited us—of course your entire population could not come at one time — you would invite us — a group or committee to visit the Earth. Our best speakers could speak to gatherings of your people in various countries of your planet. We are able to speak all languages by intuition.

There are many fine groups in your country where they are studying and learning the truth of Life. We would be welcomed by these groups and the news of our coming would spread over all the country of America. This is not wishful thinking, it is a definite plan, and it is a plan not only for the Planet Saturn but for all the planets near the Earth. There are other planets in other solar systems in other universes, farther and farther out in space. There is no end to creation. It has always been and it shall always be, expanding and growing in immensity.

We all live in our own consciousness, which is not static but constantly growing. Those who stop growing in understanding and expanding consciousness are unhappy and frustrated individuals. Those who are constantly seeking, yearning for more light, are happy individuals. This is the true nature that God gave to man on the Earth and to those who inhabit the other planets.

This does not mean that it is necessary to physically keep travelling about. Travelling physically to regions that are new to one is good. It wakens and stimulates the mind, but moving in the inner consciousness is a much greater experience. Constant expansion of consciousness is true living. "Seek and ye shall find, knock and it shall be opened unto you, ask and ye shall receive."

Yes, that is right, but do not settle down into inertia, continue seeking, knocking and asking. More and ever more understanding, greater and greater realization makes true living, joyous life. The law of life is growth. Look about you in the physical world and everywhere you will see growth.

You see plants growing from the seed; you see birds leaving the egg and growing from little naked creatures to flying singers of joyous songs. You see animals growing from helpless little creatures to activity in many forms, in forest and plane and as domesticated animals for use and for pleasure as pets. Growth is everywhere, but only the result of it is seen. The movement itself is not seen, it is invisible. God is not seen. He is invisible, but God is the living, acting cause of all that is seen, felt or experienced. God is all, there is no other.

You have grown from a baby to a grown man or woman by the action of God within you. Every little task that you perform is by the action of God. Of yourself you do nothing, God does all. It is difficult to understand and know that there is only God in existance. All is God and God is all.

We on Saturn know that—actually know it with our whole beings. Few people on the Earth have really learned that. They believe that they are separate from the Creator, living their own lives, performing their own actions. This the orthodox churches teach, just as they have for centuries, but the time has come when spiritual eyes are opening, spiritual minds and hearts are becoming active. The seed has been planted and growth is assured.

Man can look forward with assurance to a world of peace and love such as all the other planets are enjoying. But to have faith is not enough, action is required. The hearts of mankind must be opened to the action of God within. Feel the presence of God everywhere, in everything, and especially within the inner self, acting in response to your love and prayers.

This is the way we live on Saturn and it is our great desire that the people of Earth shall in the not too distant future be living thus also. If you would live like that for one day, you would make a decision to live like that forever.

We would like to visit your planet and speak in your synagogues and churches and in your advanced New Age groups. We hope that some time, not too far away, this may be accomplished. Meeting us and becoming friends with us, would make you realize that this that I am telling you is really true. You people of Earth would then feel a strong incentive to follow our example.

Your New Age groups have many large gatherings—conferences I believe they are called — where outstanding speakers are heard. We would like to be represented by one of our inspired speakers.

After listening to our speakers you may feel a stronger urge to visit our planet and spend some time travelling to our various cities, visiting our schools, our beautiful parks and recreation grounds. Also our government buildings must not be left out. You must attend a session of our legislature. I am sure you would find it interesting.

It meets in a large, handsome building in one of our cities. It is our only governing body and it makes the laws of the planet. The members of the legislative body are chosen by vote of the entire population of adults. There is no executive body, for this is not needed. All the population attend schools where these laws are studied and memorized. That is all that is needed. No one will knowingly break a law, so no police or jails are needed. All that is needed is for the people to know the laws. The law makers come together at regular intervals and review the laws. Sometimes they decide that a change should be made in one or more of them. If so, the law is written again with the change and given to the people to study.

A question may come to your mind. Are the people sometimes dissatisfied with a law? Yes, that sometimes happens, but very seldom. the people together and it is discussed, and a delegation is sent to discuss it with the legislative body. It is then decided whether to change it, keep it as it is, or eliminate it entirely.

The thought may have come to you that the cities must be very small or they could not let the whole population discuss these matters. You are right, the cities are more the size of what you call villages. The difference is not in the size but in the appearance. The buildings are large and handsome, built of the finest and most enduring materials. The schools, shops—every kind of building—is of strong, beautiful material. The only way in which villages are resembled is in the size of the population.

This small population is a great advantage, as is easily seen. The planet Saturn is a true democracy, a government of the people by the people. The planet is large, but it is divided into many small parts called cities. Each one of these is self governing. The laws are not made for the planet as a whole, any more than the laws of your country are made for the planet Earth as a whole. Remember that Saturn is a large planet. The large legislative body that I spoke of could be thought of as a body resembling the League of Nations. However, this is not a very good comparison, for the League of Nations represents separate and widely different nations, while the central legislative body on Saturn represents similar cities with populations of one blood.

Your cities in your United States each have a mayor, elected by the people, and a city council. They look after small affairs immediately concerning the city. Above the city government is the state government at the head of which is the Governor. Beyond this is the national government at the head of which is the President.

Our legislative government is very similar to this. It is our administrative government that is different. As I said before, we do not need law enforcement bodies. We do not need lawyers to argue cases or judges to decide the case. The population of each small city, or village as you might call it, has studied and learned the laws and nobody ever goes contrary to any law.

Our people live in an atmosphere of love and unselfishness. It begins in the homes and spreads out from there into all regions of the planet. How happy we would be if your Earth had an atmosphere like this.

It is not that you do not know right from wrong, but greed has taken possession of you. Greed—what a hideous thing is greed! It is seen in all parts of the Planet Earth, in all nations. Nation fights nation, race fights race, and if you look for the cause it is always greed. The stronger despoils the weaker and all over the planet there is fear and struggle. It is like the animals of the forest, where the stronger kill and devour the weaker.

When we travel over the planet Earth we see this everywhere, and our hearts ache at the sight. Almost everywhere there are churches and teachers, but sermons are listened to on Sunday and forgotten the rest of the week. It is not because of ignorance that man lives like this. If it were it could be changed by teaching. No, there is a darkness over the Earth like a pall. In this darkness there are beings of sinister purpose. It is not as if there were one Satan trying to destroy the people, no, not one but many. These are the dark spirits of greed. They have been called by different names, but by any name they are fiends. They are like vampire bats sucking the blood of the people. Some have passed out of the physical body but they are just as dangerous—maybe more dangerous—than the ones in physical bodies.

We have hesitated to speak about this for it seemed too horrible to mention. However some of your truly great Teachers are speaking, and the situation is becoming known. Some call them watchers, and some call them money-changers, but these are the same. As I have said, they are vampire bats sucking the blood of the people.

Your governing bodies do not belong to these groups. Thank God for that. We of the planet Saturn have felt forced to speak of what we see as we come close to the Earth. It is painful to do so, for this will be a great shock to the innocent hearts and minds of many.

It is known by some few groups, and the news is being spread by writing and speaking. What are these dark ones, you ask. The answer is to be found in the Apocryha of the Bible. The Aprocrypha is a part of the Bible that has been separated from the rest, being considered untrue or spurious.

It tells about the fallen angels which were driven out of heaven and, lead by Lucifer, their leader, have tempted and influenced mankind to break the commandments of God. They especially encourage greed and unbrotherly actions of all kinds; but greed predominates. With the greed is pride and conceit. Many of them are in high positions in money making organizations. These organizations are manipulated so as to make exorbitant profits for the share holders, who come from the ranks of these schemers. They came upon the Earth centuries ago and have remained, practicing their nefarious trade.

They carry on their activities in secret. On the surface they appear to be ordinary business men — very prosperous ones. We of Saturn can see them and read their minds. They are of a different breed, you might call it, from the rest of humanity, but they appear to be simply portly, ostentatious, successful business men.

In their secret meetings they show their real colors. We of the planets near the Earth can see them from our ships and also when we travel in our bodies near the Earth. We do not stay long for the atmosphere is extremely disagreeable. This atmosphere is all around the planet Earth, but the worst of it is beyond the sight of the people of Earth. The worst smog of your big cities is nothing compared to this.

These creatures and their actions have now been discovered by some of the people of the Earth and they are doing their best to make known that which they have discovered. They call themselves "The Sons of Jared," for Jared was the name of one in ancient times who exposed these demons and fought against them.

We of the other planets have decided that we should come out in the open and make this known. We would not be good friends of our brothers on Earth if we kept silent when we can see clearly what is going on. Many people have not been able to believe what has been told by the "Sons of Jared," it has seemed too fantastic and improbable. I assure you it is true, though it seems too horrible to be true. All the people of the Earth should rise up and fight against it. Not with bombs and firearms, but with words. It is now known only in the United

States of America and in only a small group there.

If you study the book of Revelation in your Bible you will find these creatures spoken of there. We, of all the other planets, urge the people of Earth to do something to stop this horror. It is not the planet Saturn alone telling you about this. Saturn is the spokesman for all the planets.

There is something that I should make clear to you. The darkness around the Earth does not come direct from these Watchers or Money Changers. No, it is from the dark forces that are attracted by them.

These dark forces are followers of Lucifer, who was once the prince of Light, but who tried to usurp the power of God Almighty and was expelled from heaven. He came to Earth with his followers and has ever since been tempting mankind in every way possible. Some human beings have not required much temptation to make them greedy and selfish; others have fought against it; others have never felt the temptation, for they loved their God with all their heart and their fellow men as themselves.

These forces of darkness know where they will be received. Some are in human form and enter into the outer events of society and into business affairs, others are invisible to the human eye. They sometimes take possession of the inner life of a man or woman.

In the New Testament of your Bible it tells how Jesus drove the evil spirits from within those who had fallen prey to them. These evil spirits, or others similar to them, are active now, in this so-called civilized age. They can be cast out now as they were in olden times, by prayer to the Father, Son and Holy Ghost.

It was said by the Master Jesus that constant vigilance was necessary, for when the evil spirit was driven out and the house was swept and garnished, it would find seven more worse than itself and enter in again, and the last state of that man would be worse than the first.

This is all literally true. It is not just a symbolic story, it is actual fact. Oh, people of Earth, wake up and look about you and when you look about do not fail to also look within, for you, unaware, may be harboring one of these evil spirits. They manifest as selfishness, greed, cruelty. They have no love for others, all their thought is centered in themselves. They are imps of Lucifer, who is on the Earth seeking whom he may destroy.

Do not be too sure that you are safe. Call on God and the Great White Brotherhood for protection. The members of the Great White Brotherhood are servants of God and instructors and guides of humanity.

You may wonder how we of another planet can know so much that you on the Earth are ignorant of. You know that often a strange visitor to a house may understand the family better than they do themselves. A certain detachment seems necessary for perfect understanding. Eyes may become dim from constantly looking on the same thing. A new scene is more easily discerned. When the true situation is seen and understood, then means of combating it may be instituted. Discussion groups should come together everywhere in all nations of the Earth.

The United States of America will be the leader of these groups. There will be groups in all the states. The people of the nation will be aroused and their minds will grasp the situation, and energy will be called forth to drive away the evil forces of darkness. This can be done by pouring forth the Light. Call for the Light of God which never fails to destroy the darkness.

Send forth love to the bewildered ones who are terrified and feel helpless. There is much for the illumined ones of Earth to do. The Great White Brotherhood has always been helping mankind by instruction and leadership. Their headquarters in America is in the Summit Lighthouse in Washington,

D.C. From there they have sent forth papers from all the great Ascended Ones.

Now they are planning to branch out into many other sections of the country, for they know that the situation is precarious all over the nation, and in fact all over the planet Earth. If the United States of America is saved much help can be given to the other countries of the Earth.

You who are reading this can help. Pray more than once or twice a day. Send forth love to all mankind. Know that God will answer your call for it has been said, "Ask and you shall receive."

This admonition has not been heeded as it should be. It should not be an ocassional asking, but daily, hourly the mind and heart should rise to the Source of all good and the call for help should go up. It need not be a long, involved prayer, a few words are all that are needed, the force of it is in the faith and love that are in the petition.

Every man, woman and child could do this. If they do, the Earth will be protected from the machinations of Lucifer and the dark forces. They cannot operate in an atmosphere of love. Wars and riots, greed and selfishness are their sustenance and strength. Deprive them of this and fill the atmosphere with love, faith in God and humanity, and the evil beings will flee away, for they will find nothing to feed on.

Do not wait, time is precious and the sooner you start to work the better. This can be done by individuals all over the Earth. It is not necessary to form groups but groups are effective for man is gregarious, and working together brings confidence, and confidence assures results.

At the present time there are large groups in Florida, New Mexico, Washington, D.C., New Zealand and in other countries. They are all sending out much light, but the help of private individuals in their own homes is greatly needed. A great sheet of light should shine all over the planet Earth so that no darkness can obscure it and no evil spirit can get through it. They are terrified and flee when the light is turned upon them.

This is the warning of the Planet Saturn, and all the other planets join with all their hearts.

With love and blessings to the Planet Earth from all her sister planets, the Planet Saturn now says farewell.

From Jupiter
The Planet of Joy

The speaker is the Ruler of a large planet to which man has given the name Jupiter. Jupiter is the name by which the ancient Romans designated the Ruler of all the Gods. The Greek name was Zeus, but it was the same God. English speaking people were more familiar with Rome than with Greece, so they used the Roman name for this planet.

Now that I have introduced myself I shall proceed to give my message. The history of this planet is not all heaven nor is it all hell. We have never fallen into the depths nor have we risen, as a people, into the celestial heights of perfection. However, I would say that there is more of heaven than of hell in our lives.

We are of one race, which makes understanding much easier than if there were many races, as there are on the Earth. We are not a very tall people as they are on Venus, but neither are we very short; I suppose we are what you would call a medium height. Also our complexion and the color of our hair is medium, it is what you call brunet. So much for our appearance.

Now for the planet on which we live. The climate varies just as the Earth's does, and for the same reason; we are not stationary, we move around the sun and we also rotate as we move. We have summer and winter, day and night, but because of the large size of the planet, the seasons are longer, as are the periods for day and night.

Our bodies are of flesh, blood, bone and muscle as yours are, and we also have a system of nerves like yours. So we feel comfortable or uncomfortable depending on the warmth or coolness of the weather, just as you do. So, indeed we are brothers and sisters of yours, and we wish to tell you so. We extend to you an invitation to visit our planet and be our guests in our homes. We could take you on a tour of the whole planet, visiting our cities and our beautiful pleasure resorts in the open country.

You would find no extreme poverty

here and no extreme wealth, for we have always been guided by moderation and a strong feeling of brotherhood. It is natural to us to be kind and generous, just as it is in a large number of your population, the difference is that with us it is all; none are greedy or cruel.

You may be wondering how I can know so much about your planet Earth. Of course you know that we can come close to the Earth in our ships of the air, but you probably do not know that without a ship we can come close to your planet, near enough to see and watch you moving about on the land and sea. Our bodies can be made light at will, so that we can travel through the air just as easily as on the land.

Our planet is one of those whose population is able to do this. I have been told that many of you Earth people, in your sleep at night, dream of flying through the air in the human body alone. This is because eons ago the people of Earth could do that, as we can now.

We all pray that the time may soon come when you, our brothers, may do that again. It is a joyous feeling to rise into the air and fly like a bird, but without the need for wings. Those that you call Angels do that. They have no wings and have no need for them. Pure joy and radiant light is all that is needed to make the body rise above the drawing power of the Earth.

It is easy and natural for you to walk upon the surface of the earth now, but when the Golden Age has arrived, once more you will be able to fly above the Earth, high in the air. There are also other forgotten abilities that shall be yours. One is the ability to precipitate solid matter from the air about you. Your saints and prophets did this centuries ago, and long before that the entire population was able to do so.

When the saints and prophets performed these acts it was considered miraculous, but thousands of years before it was as simple and natural as eating or drinking. We on Jupiter still find it so, and we would be very happy to instruct our brothers and sisters of Earth in this, to us, simple art. Food, drink and clothing can be created this way, so no one need be hungry or cold.

You, dear ones of Earth, have lost the ability to do these things because ages ago you forgot the Source of all life, from which all creation flows forth. Some of your churches still sing a beautiful little hymn, "Praise God from whom all blessings flow, praise Him all creatures here below, praise Him above Ye heavenly host, praise Father, Son and Holy Ghost."

This is sung, but the words do not have their true meaning deep in the heart. It has been forgotten and no longer is known—or rather felt instinctively —that God only performs all actions. The word God, as used here, means the Great Power which is the Source of all that is, was, or ever shall be. Mankind forgot and wandered away from the Source of All Being, giving himself, the little human self, all the credit for his accomplishments.

The little human self has never had the ability to perform any act, even the simplest. Not even an arm can be raised without the power of God within. This is done without doubt, and is learned in innocent babyhood. It is true that the baby does not think as an adult thinks, and in this fact is the joy and beauty of the infant's life. He moves his arms and legs by instinct and there is no doubt felt. Every motion that he makes is developing the muscles of his little body. These movements are joy to him, and pure joy is health. He feels the love of his parents and love for them is born in him.

Like this was man in the beginning. He lived by instinct, as the birds and animals do. Joy was in his being—the joy of life. He did not doubt, but lived life as it came to him. When he began to think, he also began to doubt. Why were thinking and doubting connected? Because he had lost the deep feeling of oneness with the source of all life and was living on the surface. In his thinking he was mistaken, he believed that each human being was a separate entity, living his own life by his own power.

Before he began to think he felt, deep within his being, the truth of life, and knew, without trying to reason, that there was a greater power than his own little self acting within and through him. He did not try to reason, he simply felt that this was so.

At the present time on Earth another change has come to vast numbers of people; they both think that which is true, and feel it in the depths of their being. Now man feels his oneness with God, the Creator, and also understands in his mind.

We of Jupiter rejoice with mankind, for we for many eons have understood, and practiced that which we understood and felt. Life should be pure joy, and is when it is understood and accepted as it is. What is it? It is love, pure divine love. Centuries ago this was taught on the planet Earth, but it was accepted in the lives and living of a comparatively small number, the others believed in force and force is still, at this present time, being practiced all over the Earth.

Dear brothers of Earth, open your hearts and your eyes and join the other planets in living lives of peace, not conflict.

This writing was not intended to be a sermon, but perhaps it seems to be one. I hope it will not be misunderstood. We of the planet Jupiter extend to you a most cordial invitation to visit us, and we will be most happy to come to the Earth in our ships of the air, and carry you to our planet for a visit to all the places of interest and beauty. Above all we would like you to meet us in our homes, and have friendly chats with us.

Speaking for all the inhabitants of the Planet Jupiter, I, Jupiter give you of Earth our sincere love and friendship.

Invitation From The Planet Venus

This is coming to you from Venus and is dictated by the Ruler of Venus, who also is named Venus, the Goddess of Love. I have always been the ruler of this planet and always shall be, for such is the law. One ruler who is satisfactory to the people, and who lives forever.

Many of you may not believe this, for on the planet Earth every human body dies, though the spirit in that body lives forever in a higher plane of consciousness. The human body becomes old and worn out, or becomes sick and destroyed by disease. This does not take place on Venus.

The planet Venus is our home now and shall be forever. We are happy in our lives, living in love and perfect unselfishness. Everything on our planet might be called perfect. At the present time this cannot be said of the planet Earth. It is a common saying, "nothing is perfect." Some earnest ones are called perfectionists, for they always aim at perfection, and sometimes do attain it. There are inventions which are acting perfectly, but most of them could be improved.

One of these inventions is your airplane. It is wonderful that man, after the struggle of centuries, has produced a ship of the air that flies easily and very rapidly the greatest distances on the planet. The fuel gasoline is used and it is used in your automobiles also. A machine using this fuel moves as rapidly and as far in distance as anyone could desire, but there is one flaw which is very serious. Very noxious fumes pour from the vehicles.

These fumes are injurious to the health of the inhabitants of the Earth, human, animal and vegetable. There is a way to prevent these fumes, and that is, do not use gasoline.

We who live on other planets near the planet Earth get our fuel from the atmosphere. Your scientists could learn this from the other planets if you would become friends and accept our offer. I briefly touch on this and we now return to the planet Venus.

Those of you who have studied the mythology of Greece and Rome know that the names of the planets were taken from the names of Gods and Goddesses of the Greek and Roman religion. In your Earth thinking and belief in this century, this religion is only myth or fairy tale, and you may be shocked when I say that it is truth.

I am the Venus who was called the Goddess of love and beauty, but there is a difference in the meaning of these terms "love and beauty." They, on the Earth, have lost their true meaning of pure, spiritual Love and pure, spiritual Beauty, and are used with the meaning of physical beauty and sensuous love.

As I have already told you, the people of Venus are very happy and contented. All put others before themselves, give with joy and receive with gratitude. It is an ideal life and there is no reason that it may not last forever.

Now it is our greatest desire to help the inhabitants of the Earth to understand and know the possibility of living such a life. With us it is not a beautiful dream of the distant future, it is a present fact. This can become a fact on the planet Earth, but education must come first.

Man must be taught, as children are taught in school. It is necessary to learn first what can be, by knowing what already is on the neighboring planets.

It is not an impossibility for the Earth people to live perfect lives of joy and perfection, but it will require first of all a sincere desire to attain this perfection. Before desire there must be belief that this can be, and that it already is in other places. This we are trying to show you by giving ourselves as examples.

The base of our civilization rests on a strong love and worship of the One Great Source of all life, the One God above all Gods, the Creator and Sustainer of all life. God is Life, God is Love, God is Light. God is everywhere, in everything, from the tiniest blade of grass to the Universe of Universes.

Many of you Earth people know this and rejoice in the knowledge, but there are more who do not know it. They believe in a God outside of creation, in a heaven far away in the sky, a severe God who punishes His children for their sins and mistakes.

A God such as this never existed. We of Venus have always known the truth and loved with all our hearts the God of Love, in whom is all life, love and power. Without Him nothing would be, for all is in Him and He is in all.

It is very difficult if not impossible to express the truth, for God is not a being that can be called He, nor can this being be called she. Recently the words Father-Mother have been used in an effort to express the truth, but they fail to express it.

The great Source of all life is formless. Being everywhere, how could it have a form? It is in every living thing, in insects, birds, beasts, human beings, plants and even stones; it is in the air, water, soil.

It is consciousness everywhere and we live in that consciousness. We are all formed in that consciousness, live and have our being in it. It is All. There is nothing else anywhere, in anything. It is impossible to express this, although It is expression, everywhere expressing everything.

It expresses in forms, your forms, our forms, all forms. The cause of the forms is formless. No words can express the truth of life, but the human heart can love and adore that which the human mind is unable to express. The truth can be felt even though it cannot be expressed. This is so everywhere, in all the planets, in all the universes, in the great everywhere without beginning, without end, which it is impossible for any mind to grasp.

But though our minds cannot grasp this truth our hearts can and do love it. It is our great desire that not only a few of Earth's people, as now, know this truth, but that every individual on the planet Earth may know and rejoice in it.

When this is so there will be peace instead of war, plenty instead of poverty. There will be love instead of harsh criticism and dislike. As the wise of the Earth have already told you "peace must begin with me"—with each one. From there it will flow out to all mankind. Not only to all mankind, but to animals also. No longer will there be shooting of deer and birds for pleasure—sport it is called. The American Indians were above doing this, they killed by necessity, for they had not learned to raise enough grain on which to sustain life. It was necessary for them to eat meat, but they never killed for sport.

The machine age has played a good part in freeing horses and oxen from the drudgery of hard work under the whips of their owners. How we of Venus rejoiced when we saw this take place.

I feel a thrill of surprise in the one who is writing this, and from this judge that those who read may also be startled to know that we can look at the planet Earth and see quite clearly what is going on in the fields and on the streets.

We also have instruments, and very good ones. You call your instruments for long distance seeing, telescopes. We have a different name in our language but it means the same. These instruments are very efficient and we can look onto the planet Earth and see much of that which is going on.

We do not intrude on your privacy by looking into your houses, but that which is in the open we can see. We shall be willing and pleased when you can see what we are doing in our fields and streets. You will then no longer be afraid of us. You will see that we are beings like yourselves. We have our shops, business offices and places of entertainment. We love music and art of all kinds. We play games of skill and dexterity but never games that become battles as some of yours do.

We are your friends, as the inhabitants of all the planets are, and our great desire is that you may visit us and see for yourselves how we live and what kind of beings we are. Only close contact can give you a true knowledge of our lives. This writing can give you information. It can dispel wrong beliefs and replace them with the truth, but only meeting us and knowing us can give you realization of what we truly are.

To realize you must enter into our actual everyday lives, meet our little children as well as our statesmen and business men. You must see our beautiful flowers and trees, our lakes and streams, our sunshine and showers.

We invite you to come and experience all this with us. Some few of you have actually been taken into a space ship and brought here, but most of these have not been in the physical body. They have travelled in the etheric body, leaving the physical on the Earth. This is good but not quite the same as coming in your physical bodies, for we are in physical bodies, living and carrying on all our affairs in physical bodies. So you can understand that in order to have a perfectly natural contact you should come to us in physical bodies.

You can do that if you are willing to board one of our ships of the air, and trust us to bring you to our planet. Then, after your visit, we would return you to the Earth. This would be done with each planet. But, as I explained before, if you learn to build your own space craft you could travel from planet to planet in perfect freedom.

We shall now continue on our imaginary visit to the planet Venus. Our lives are not entirely different from yours. In fact, they are quite similar to yours in many respects. The one great difference is that we live entirely in love—pure, divine love. There are no quarrels, no destructive criticism, all is peace and true love. I was about to say brotherly love, but on the Earth brothers, even though they may love each other, often have relapses, when they quarrel and have very bitter, unbrotherly feelings. On Venus this is never so. Even the tiny tots never quarrel.

This is the great difference between our planets. To the outer vision there is not so much difference in what you shall see. We have cities, farms, mountains, plains, all quite similar to yours at a casual glance, but on investigation a great difference is found.

We have no slums, no poverty anywhere. Also there is no extreme wealth. All the people are living in comfort and in pleasant surroundings. The cities are not devoid of trees and flowers. Our large cities are not crowded, but are spread over enough territory to comfortably accommodate the population. There are many play grounds for the children, so they do not have to play on the streets and sidewalks.

But there is something that is better than these outer things, and that is a serene inner joy that is felt by every living being. This peace and love that is felt by every person goes forth into the atmosphere and is felt by animals and birds. The peace of God which is in the center of every living thing.

Spiritual ones on the earth feel it, not always perhaps, but at times. It is a peace that prevails over all emotions of worry, doubt or fear. It is serene and joyful. Divine love for all creation brings the peace of God which is triumphant over all emotions. When you enter our large cities this is felt as strong as in the open country, or in the forests or mountains. This is not so on the Earth. There men seek the great open spaces to find peace and rest. Those of you who have gone into these quiet places on your planet will know of what I

But there is something that is better than these outer things, and that is a serene inner joy that is felt by every living being. This peace and love that is felt by every person goes forth into the atmosphere and is felt by animals and birds. The peace of God which is in the center of every living thing.

Spiritual ones on the earth feel it, not always perhaps, but at times. It is a peace that prevails over all emotions of worry, doubt or fear. It is serene and joyful. Divine love for all creation brings the peace of God which is triumphant over all emotions. When you enter our large cities this is felt as strong as in the open country, or in the forests or mountains. This is not so on the Earth. There men seek the great open spaces to find peace and rest. Those of you who have gone into these quiet places on your planet will know of what I terest on the Earth because of reports in the newspapers concerning the discussions and theories of scientists. Some very powerful instruments are now in use which have given more information than has ever been had before concerning the planet Mercury.

We shall not discuss the theories and speculations of the scientists. Our effort shall be devoted to persuading mankind to accept the friendship of the inhabitants of the planets in the solar system in which the Earth rotates. We know that we are living beings just as you know that you are living beings. There is no theory or speculation about it. It is the truth.

All the planets will send more space ships of various kinds onto the Earth in order to attract the attention of more and more people. We are very well informed concerning the geography of the Earth, and we know where the open spaces suitable for landing are located.

There is little more to be said in this writing. One thing more, we have not yet described our personal looks. What do we look like? We have faces and bodies like yours but there are differences, which I will mention. We are a very tall people and all of us are golden blonds with blue eyes. We have not the variety that you have of blond, brunette or red-head, nor are there great differences in height as there is on Earth. No one is much under six feet and many are well over that.

You may think that this would be monotonous but we are used to it and do not notice any monotony, for each is an individual mentally and spiritually, even though we have hair of the same color.

To us who live on Venus the inner expression of individuals is very much more important than the outer form of body, face or hair.

I, Venus, speaking for the people of Venus, now say farewell to the Earth and another will take my place. We send you our love and our blessings.

Planet Mercury Sends Greetings

This is the second in a series of writings concerning the space ships of the planets in the solar system of which the Earth is part. I shall give you my name and the name of the planet that I rule. It is one and the same, Mercury. It is not a strange name to mankind, for centuries ago it was known to man as the name of One who was called the messenger of the Gods. He wore a cap, on each side of which were wings, and on his feet were wings, while in his hand he carried a staff around which a serpent was wound.

He moved very swiftly through the air carrying messages from one God to another in the solar system. The earth people of that day knew nothing of solar systems. They thought that the earth was flat and the stars, moon, and sun moved above it; but they did have some information concerning the Gods and Goddesses above the earth, although much of their belief was erroneous.

At the present time on Earth, man is also mistaken concerning the other planets about the Earth. To him they have been uninhabited, and the stories told about the Gods and Goddesses have been only fables, charming and beautiful subjects for the pictures of great artists, or for statues and beautiful poems. They were not believed to be fact—real, living beings.

I can assure you that they are real, living Beings, and always have been such. The Earth is only a small planet in a system of planets which is called the Solar System. It is one Solar System among many in the Universe and the Universe is one Universe among many Universes. I, who speak to you, am the God or Ruler of the planet Mercury, which has my name. It is a small planet very close to the earth. You may be disappointed to know that I do not have wings on my cap or on my heels, nor do I carry the caduceus. I do not need these to fly with. I can fly through space without the assistance of any wings or mechanical aid. I do, however, at times use a space craft in order to have with me others from my planet. It is the same as people on Earth traveling together.

The space craft that we use are not all alike, there are a number of shapes and sizes. The first that modern men saw with the sun shining on them, looked round and concave, so they called them flying saucers. They were not exactly the shape they appeared to be as they moved swiftly over the Earth. Later, others were seen which were long and "cigar shaped." These long ones were seen to land on the earth and discharge smaller ships of a different shape. Some were round and some the shape of a mushroom.

It has been said—and truly—that hundreds of space ships flew over Washington, D.C. at one time. Many people saw them, but the government has always suppressed the news of the appearance of these craft. More and more individuals have been seeing them, usually over open space, plains, and flat prairies, though occasionally over the mountains, or even over, and close to, a city street. The visits of these craft are no secret, try though the government may to make it so.

There is also a plan which no inhabitant of Earth can stop—and it is for the benefit of the inhabitants of Earth—and that is for a series of writings such as this. One little book from each planet. This is the second one, and one by one the others shall follow. This one shall deal with Mercury.

Our planet is small, but it is throbbing with life and activity. The climate is mild and beautiful. The air is pure and clean for there are no poisonous sprays used, there are no fumes given off from our vehicles, in which the people travel from place to place on the planet, or from the great space ships which carry us from planet to planet.

This can no longer be said of our sister planet, the Earth. Not so very long ago the air of the Earth was as pure as ours, but alas, it is now dense with fumes which are called smog. But the readers of this book know too well that this is so. We shall now turn our attention entirely to the planet Mercury.

The government might be called paternal, for one ruler is always at the head of it, but you might call it fraternal for the people discuss and decide many things—in fact almost all of the laws that govern the planet, for laws are necessary in any civilization. There is only one race on the planet and all is one nation. I must admit that this makes government much simpler than it is on Earth.

The weather is not the same evenly all over the surface of the planet. Heat and cold vary from one location to another. Most of the planet has what you would call a moderate climate, while some parts are warmer, and others cooler.

Farming is carried on with success in most locations, and even the cities have gardens of beautiful flowers, and the streets are all lined with trees. This can be found in many places on your Earth even now, but the cities are becoming bleaker as the population increases and in many of them trees and flowers are not found.

I feel sure you would enjoy a visit to Mercury, and you would be welcomed most cordially and taken on tours of the planet. We have many very fine hotels, where you would find comfortable and beautiful rooms for the guests, and most delicious food. Those who greeted you would be your hosts, and your tour of the planet would cost you nothing. You would be sure to have a happy time, and would see nothing to rouse your sympathy and make you unhappy, as is the case when touring certain parts of the Earth.

There is no poverty on Mercury and no excessive wealth. There are no classes of highly educated, and ignorant. All are educated and intelligent. This may be almost beyond your imagination, but it is the truth. I shall tell you what is the cause of this idyllic life.

It is what the angels sang to the Earth on the day that Christ was born, "Glory to God in the highest and on Earth peace, goodwill toward men." We on Mercury live this in our daily lives. Our hearts sing always, "Glory to God and love to our fellows." We feel that all of us are brothers and all are equal. All have equal rights, there is no privileged class or underprivileged class. No one is hungry for anything, either physical or spiritual.

We of Mercury are looking forward expectantly to the time when the scientists of Earth shall have accepted our help in constructing a space ship such as ours. Then the people of Earth can come to us as we now go to them. They can fly easily and quietly from planet to planet visiting, and accepting our brotherly hospitality. For we feel that we are your brothers and sisters—we know that we are.

It makes our hearts ache to see the cruelty and greed of the Earth people and their destructive treatment of the planet, which was so beautiful. Our hearts never ache for anyone on our planet for all is peace and happiness.

We can hear you asking, "Has this always been the condition on Mercury?" The answer is, "No, we passed through a very unhappy period, very similar to that which the Earth is going through at the present time. Some individuals who were in business—for there were businesses of various kinds — looked about at their fellows and thought of ways to take advantage of them, thus accumulating more money, with which to buy luxuries for themselves at the expense of their trusting clients.

This was the beginning of a situation such as you have on Earth at present. We forgot God, from whom all blessings flow, and thought only of ourselves. Some were grasping, so others retaliated, and thus began a long period of time in which we lived as you on Earth are living now. Some of the people lived in great luxury, while others had not enough food to nourish their bodies, and not enough good clothing to keep them warm. This condition became worse, until I, who was the supreme Ruler of the planet, and the ones who had advisory positions in the government, realized that something must be done to stop and change this deplorable situation.

So we met together and went into the stillness of deep meditation, opening our hearts and minds to receive the instruction which came to us from the Life within us, which flowed from the Source of all that Is. Then we saw clearly where the trouble lay.

We called on all the leaders in every town and hamlet to do as we had done; get together in deep meditation and let the Life, or God, within them give them the answer, for when they in this way understood, and could see what was the cause of the trouble, they then would receive inspiration from the Voice within them directing them in the proper procedure. It was necessary to warn the people of the danger which threatened the whole planet because of the greed and selfishness of a few individuals, which was spreading like a disease and drawing more and more active business into these nefarious practices.

Fortunately for our planet there were no large cities but many small towns. The governing officials of each town called a meeting, explained the situation, and warned the people of the danger to the population as a whole because of the greed of a few.

They lifted their hearts in prayer to the Great Source of all Being, which was the Life within each one of them. They prayed for guidance, and it was received and followed. Many illumined Souls on Earth have individually practiced this in their own lives, meditating daily, or oftener, several times a day, raising their consciousness into the spiritual realm and receiving the answer, which changed perplexity into certainty, and a clear course of procedure was followed. This which has been done, and is being done by individuals in their private lives, can be also followed in the government of cities and countries.

The officials of the government could follow this plan, and the individual citizens could call for the blessing and help of the Great Source of all Life, to open the hearts and minds of both leaders and followers, so that wisdom would be the guide. Wisdom and love always go hand in hand.

You who are reading this can practice this in your own lives, for yourselves and for your government. Send forth love over all the Earth, bless all the nations, beginning with your own private life, then your country, and finally all the Earth.

This is the way the planet Mercury was saved from the extremes of poverty and wealth, from greed and brutality, and war. We can advise you people of the Planet Earth because we have saved ourselves from a like condition. We are grateful, when we look into the Planet Earth and see the misery and crime there, that we are able to give the nations and the individuals the true story of our own experience. What we have done you can do. It may be more difficult, because the remedy has not been applied as soon as we did, but it can be done.

At the present time we see a tremendous uplift among the inhabitants of Earth. Light is shining in the darkness and is spreading fast from the United States of America, where freedom was the aim of the Founding Fathers of the country. Their example has not been followed by those who came after them and there is much poverty and crime in the country but the spark that they lit has never died, and now it is growing in size and brightness.

In the midst of the turmoil and the horrors in the world of the Earth, a great power for good is increasing, fed by the love and devotion of thousands—no, millions of dedicated ones. They are those who have been receiving the New Age Teaching, and who are practicing that which they have learned and believe with all their hearts.

Saint Germain was the instigator of this movement, which is spreading over the Earth, but Jesus the Christ, who came onto the Earth centuries ago and gave his life for mankind, was the savior of mankind, at a period of time when it seemed that mankind and the Earth itself must perish.

There are many forms of this teaching, many leaders and many groups. It may seem strange that One from another planet should tell you this, but sometimes a stranger sees more clearly, and without any of the prejudice that has handicapped those living in the midst of a situation.

All these active groups are guided by Teachers from the Great White Brotherhood, though some of them do not know this. They have fanned the spark of brotherly love that still smouldered on the Earth, and we can now see the light brightening and spreading in many parts of the Earth, but especially in the United States of America.

In earlier days the oppressed citizens of other countries fled to America in search of freedom, and there they settled and made it their home. But, alas, those who had fled from persecution began to persecute others of different religions, who had followed them. At that time there were only separate colonies on the Western continent, all settled by people who had come in search of freedom to worship God according to their belief.

But the beliefs of the people who sought freedom differed in minor ways and, as it had been in Europe, it now was in America, the stronger persecuted the weaker and there was no freedom that was universal.

There still is no true freedom anywhere on the Planet Earth. But the love of freedom and the desire for it has never died. The light is shining in the darkness and increasing, not diminishing. We can see that very distinctly.

A glorious future is destined for the Planet Earth. Those who are prophets can see it, and they are not few, but man himself must awake to the situation and become active. Anyone with ordinary intelligence can see that wars should cease, crime should cease, poverty should not be, cheating and chicanery should not exist.

The papers are full of distressing accounts of robbery, murder and rape in the cities, and war between the smaller nations in which the larger nations are implicated. But the population as a whole makes no effort to remedy the condition.

On every coin that is used by the people these words are clearly stamped, Liberty, In God We Trust, and E Pluribus Unum which means, From Many One. These words were in the hearts and minds of the founders of the nation and every child has heard them.

Now in this century of the Earth a great movement is spreading, beginning in the United States of America and spreading out in all directions to all parts of the globe. Groups of people are coming together to worship God, whose love and power are the basis of all creation. There are different ways in the various groups, of receiving and giving forth, that which in every case comes from the Great Spirit which is the cause of all life, love and peace.

Some groups practice decreeing, which is a repetition of phrases full of love, demanding cleansing of the Earth and its inhabitants, and replacing that which is untrue and destructive with Love and Truth. Other groups come together to receive teaching from Great Masters who speak through the leaders of the groups.

Besides the many groups there are individuals who are receiving the words of Truth from the higher realms of Life, and writing them to send out to all who are searching for Truth and illumination. There are many who are searching, and many who have found, for the time is now ripe. This small writing is given in that way. I, Mercury, receive the thought and the words from a higher Source, and the one who does the manual writing receives the words from me. It is very simple. With this writing much love is given, for love is that which accomplishes all good works. When there is love there is also light, and wisdom and joy are the result. The foundation of all is complete faith in the living Source of all, which in most countries is called God.

Whatever word may be used to designate this great force, it is one and the same force. That which is life everywhere, and love everywhere, expressing in all forms and creations. Life is the foundation, and love is the key, to all that is constructive, and we must not forget faith, which encourages and strengthens those who work in the vineyard of life. Faith is very necessary.

Beloved ones who read this little booklet. You are seekers for the Truth of life. Your hearts are full of love for humanity. Have faith in the Great Power which guides the destiny of every living being, be it man or little bird. The birds build their nests and raise their young ones by unthinking faith. Men accomplish marvels by thinking faith.

All great inventors have faith. Their faith is strong and unyielding. Disappointment after disappointment is conquered, and faith is still strong in their hearts. Sometimes the one who began the work does not succeed, but the work is taken up where he left off, by another worker in another generation.

All mankind is one. No one lives alone. It may seem so on the surface, but within all is one life. One energy pours through the whole; one great power, the power of love, holds all together as one.

This we on the Planet Mercury have learned by hard and bitter experience, for we had sunk to the depths as you on the Earth have done. Greed, war and destruction were rampant all over our planet. It became so bad that something had to be done. There is a saying on the Earth, "Mans extremity is God's opportunity."

This is true, and in desperation we turned to God for help. When I say we, I am speaking of the population of the planet and all, both population and ruler are one. I had done all I could to reach the hearts and minds of the people, and make them understand what was happening because of their greed. But they would not listen until they were in extremity.

Then they stopped, looked and listened. Then they asked for help. They raised their minds to the Source of their beings and prayed for help in their desperation, and help came. The Lord of all creation answered their prayers as He always does when prayers are sincere and unselfish. All troubles can be overcome by honest, sincere prayer. We urge man to listen to us and follow our example, for the result was even beyond our expectation.

Now you know why the people of the Planet

Mercury are living lives of complete happiness, with plenty of the material goods necessary for physical sustenance, and all the beauty and joy of spiritual life.

Now that you have read this and understand something of the history of this planet, the next thing is for you to accept our invitation and visit us. When you travel over our planet, as our guests, visiting our towns, our factories, schools, libraries, and most important our private homes, you will be ready, when you return to the planet Earth, to begin in earnest to follow our example.

Theory alone is worthless, practice is needed in order to bring results. But before the people of Earth are ready to accept what I have been telling them and practice it on their planet, they must let us take their leaders in our ships to our planet as our visitors.

I will give you an idea of what is to be seen on our beautiful planet. Remember, it is a small planet and there is only one nation and one race. Our ship shall go directly to the capitol. It is a beautiful building, but not more beautiful than your capitol at Washington, D.C. We enter and find nothing very different from your capitol.

We leave and go to a court of law where a trial is under way. Here there is a striking difference. There is a judge and a jury but there are no lawyers. There are two men who have had a disagreement concerning a piece of property—about the boundary line between two homes. Each one was given an opportunity to speak, without interruption. A stenographer took down all that was said. Then the judge and the jury withdrew to another room which is called, "The room of consultation." There they discussed the situation, by first carefully reading the stenographic record, and then any member of the jury who wished to speak raised his hand and the judge called his name. He gave his opinion, which was taken down by the stenographer. If another disagreed, he was recognized by the judge, and he spoke.

This was continued until everyone who wished to express his opinion had done so. There was no oratory or flowery language, no effort to put either of the contestants in a bad light. All were calm and quiet in giving their opinions.

We with our visitors do not wait until the case is decided, for it will take some time to read all the records of the jurors opinions. When all these have been studied the judge will give the deciding verdict. There has been no verbal fighting, no oratory, only quiet expressions of opinion. The judge is well versed in the law, for there are laws which are scrupulously followed. Sometimes, if there have been many contrary opinions by the jurors, it may be several days before the judge gives his verdict.

Now we shall get into our conveyance and go to another small town. We are not traveling in a space ship, but in a conveyance not very different in appearance from your automobile. However, there are differences. The fuel, like that of the space ship is drawn from the atmosphere and there are no noxious fumes pouring into the air. We drive out into the country over smoothly paved roads. There are beautiful trees, grass, and flowers in all directions. In the distance we see mountains whose tops are capped with snow. We pass through several small towns. The people live in pretty little houses, each individually planned. In front and around each there are flowers, and behind there are sometimes vegetables and fruit trees. Much of your own planet used to be like this, but there is not much like it now.

There is no large city anywhere on the planet Mercury. Even in these small towns there are parks and playgrounds for children. Of course there are schools and shops. Everywhere the air is pure and sparkling and the sky blue, for it is not raining on the day we take you to visit us. We do have rain at times for without it the planet would be a desert. We have learned how to draw the clouds and produce rain when it is needed. It is said that your American Indians can do this, and the white people have occasionally brought rain from clouds that have gathered, but it is not regularly practiced.

There are not many restaurants or hotels in our towns, usually one of each, for that is enough to accommodate the travelers who are passing through. Our party goes to one of the hotels and finds it clean and comfortable. In another town we eat at the restaurant and find the food not very different from that to which you are accustomed.

But we have invitations from several families, in different towns, who would like you to be their guests for a day and a night. You spend a day and a night with each one. Some of them have young children, others are older persons and have what you on Earth call teen-agers. You have pleasant conversations with all these families, you eat their food, and you enter into some of their games and pastimes. They treat you like old friends, and you feel perfectly at ease and return their friendship.

We could fly easily from this planet and tour another planet but the plan for you is different. Your trips will all originate on the Earth and go to another planet each time, not from one planet to another. In this way you can judge the distance each planet is from your home planet, the Earth.

We all have strong hopes that you will accept our offer to teach you how to build a space ship like ours, so that you may travel from planet to planet and tour the entire solar system in a leisurely way. It will be like the tour of Europe, Asia or Africa that some of you fortunate ones make, not like a hasty guided tour of a few weeks, catching hasty glimpses of noted art galleries or beautiful scenery.

No, the plan is for you to linger long enough to really know the people and customs of each planet and make friends in each one. With your own ship you could do this. You could engage guides as you go from place to place. These would be professional guides such as there are in the countries of the Earth. They would know the history of the nation and all the places of interest.

planet and make friends in each one. With your own ship you could do this. You could engage guides as you go from place to place. These would be professional guides such as there are in the countries of the Earth. They would know the history of the nation and all the places of interest.

They would relieve you of all the troublesome part of travel, but you would not have to hurry, you could stay as long as you wished when you were interested, and if you were not interested, move on.

If you landed on a planet and found at once that you did not like it, you could enter your ship and be on your way to the next planet.

This is a carefully thought out plan, not only by the rulers of the planets, but by the Great White Brotherhood, which has communication with the people of Earth whose minds are open to them. They can prepare the minds of their students so that they can receive telepathic communication direct from us.

Any one of you could receive messages if you had the desire to do so and the love which would give the incentive. When you pray to your Father in heaven, you are both the sender and the receiver of a telepathic message. There is nothing supernatural about it, it is entirely natural.

We are also communicating with you by visiting you in our space ships. Many of you have seen these ships and some of you have conversed with those who are in them. There have even been instances when the Earth man has been taken on board and shown over the vessel, or in a few cases, actually taken to visit a planet. People are losing their fear and many are becoming very much interested in the ships which hover over the Earth or land upon it.

How beautiful the Earth could be, for it was very beautiful when it was a new creation. Think of the most beautiful landscape you have ever seen and imagine all of the Earth like that. All was like one big, glorified park. Man was put on this beautiful planet, told to increase and multiply, and to care for the Earth, the plants and animals.

Alas, the demon greed entered in, and now the soil is being poisoned and the animals and birds killed. Greed is the worst sin there is. It is the opposite to love. Love never destroys, it is always constructive. It is the cause of great inventions, beautiful pictures, delightful music; everything that brings happiness and peace. Greed is a destroyer and causes war and poverty.

We on the planet Mercury know this, not only in our minds, but in our whole beings, for we have experienced it ourselves. That is why we are so very anxious to warn our brothers on the planet Earth, and to urge them to listen to us, for we know that of which we are speaking.

Our love and blessings are always with the people of Earth, for we are all the children of the One Great Creator.

Three Undiscovered Planets

This writing comes from a planet that has not been discovered by the powerful instruments of the astronomers. This planet is one of three which are not far from the planet Earth but are invisible to human eye, even when looking through telescopes. The reason for this is because the planet and the inhabitants of the planet are not in flesh, as those who have communicated with you so far are. We are in etheric bodies, as are the souls of those who leave the physical body in so-called death.

I can assure you, however, that we are just as much alive as you are, really more alive. We are not ever troubled by sickness or weariness. We never tire. Our minds are keen and our hearts are full of love. We can travel any distance without a machine of any kind. In other words, our lives are lives of perfection.

You may wonder, then, how we can give ourselves as examples of living to the people of Earth. The planets that have spoken before are populated by those in physical bodies. They are living lives of happiness and peace and it makes them sad to see the tumult on the Earth, the struggle and war among nations, the greed among individuals.

I must admit that we, in our present state, cannot offer ourselves as examples to man, but we were centuries ago flesh and blood beings just as you are. We were sinful, greedy and grasping. Our bodies became sick, tired and weary, and we fought battles between nations and even civil wars within a nation.

Now all of us have passed through that which has been ignorantly called death. There is no death, only transition from one state of life to another.

We are all now in etheric bodies, which is another name for spiritual bodies. Our lives are entirely lives of love and peace. This does not mean that our lives are dull and uninteresting, far from it. Our lives are full of interest and activity.

This which I am doing now, writing to the planet Earth, is interesting and new to me. It is the first time I have spoken to an inhabitant of the Earth, so it is very interesting to me. On our own planet, even though it is my home, I am always finding something new and interesting. So never think that a life of peace and love must be dull.

Unhappiness, struggle and conflict are lacking and we are thankful that they are. The people of Earth could and can attain this peace and love, for within their physical bodies, spirit resides, and spirit is the true Self which lives forever. It is the Source of all Being. Spirit is the fountain of life where one may drink and live forever. Our great Teachers have taught us this, and we believe and within us *know* that this is true.

You people of Earth had a great Teacher who preached and lived this truth. He lived centuries ago and his name was Jesus. Many on Earth love him, but very few keep his precepts. We see the Earth in war and tumult, thousands suffering from famine; starving in the cities and in the open country; marching in protest and revolt; destroying, stealing, killing.

How can this be? We would not believe that it could be true if we did not see it with our own eyes. We are able to see all that goes on at all times on our sister planet, Earth. Why do we speak of the other planets as "sister" instead of "brother"? Because the planets themselves are gentle, peaceful and loving no matter what the population may be.

Perhaps you have never known that a planet in itself is a living being, feeling, sensitive, loving. This is the truth. There is nothing in form anywhere that does not have life and feeling. In some forms the feeling is very dull, scarcely perceptible, in other forms, keen.

The planets are Beings of love and their feelings are keen. Their lives are passive. The lives of the inhabitants are not passive, they are very active, but they express peace, beauty and joy. They never do anything to destroy or injure the planet on which they live. The fauna of the planet is never destroyed, the animals are never killed.

Yes, there are animals, beautiful and gentle, and there are trees and flowers of great variety. There are mountains and valleys, lakes, streams and oceans. To look down from a distance and see this, one cannot see much difference from the planet Earth. Looking closer, however; there can be seen a great difference. There are no barren dry spaces where trees have once been. There are no deserts where the temperature is excessively hot, nor any place where the temperature is excessively cold.

Gentleness and peace reign everywhere. So it has been created, and so it remains. There are no wild beasts of prey. The animals are gentle, the birds sing and fly as yours do, but there are none preying on the smaller birds or little animals.

All living beings are Spirit, there are no beings of flesh and blood. This may seem very strange to the readers of these words, for to you

Spirit is always invisible, that is, to the vast majority of the population; there are a few who are clairvoyant —clear seeing—who see at times the forms of the spirits.

Spirit is the pure essence of Life, proceeding from the Source of all Being. Flesh is only the container of Spirit. The body has been called the tabernacle of the Spirit. As such, it should be cared for and never abused. We who are without flesh, nevertheless have form, and our forms resemble those of perfect men and women.

You all probably know that when a human being leaves the physical body he still has form, but the form is spirit, not flesh. He leaves the Earth for a higher sphere. It is easy to understand. With us, eons ago the entire population left the physical body, and the planet likewise abandoned the physical and existed only in the spiritual. It may seem very strange to you, but it can be understood. 163

There are three planets now living in spirit only and they are not very far from the planet Earth. Our planets, not being seen, have not been named by man. We have our own names in our own languages, for we have found it convenient to have language although we read minds usually.

Names are given for convenience, just as they are on Earth. The name of the planet on which I live is the name of a very beautiful flower which grows and blooms in profusion all over our planet. There is no way of giving it to you. It is the same with the other two planets; their names could not be spoken or written in your language or any other language.

The names are expressive of beauty in form, radiance and perfume. They are not all flowers, but they are all beautiful expressions of Life. We regret that we are unable to give these names to our sister planet Earth.

The writing of this booklet will be shared by all three planets, for though we are separate and individual our experience is similar and there would be nothing different to tell you.

All are planets of spirit living similar lives of love and happiness. Many of you on Earth receive communication from advanced Souls who speak to you from a plane above the Earth. They are in etheric bodies, though they have been men and women on the Earth.

The only difference in this communication is that I who speak have never been in physical body for it has been many eons in time since this planet and its inhabitants were in physical bodies. It is the same with the other two planets. Now I shall bid you beloved ones of Earth farewell and allow the other speakers to have their say.

This is the speaker of the next planet which is in spiritual form. There is nothing that I can add to my brother's talk. We are as like as two peas in a pod.—You see we pick up some of your sayings.—This is only to say greetings and farewell and to assure you that we are your friends and well-wishers. I shall step aside and allow the brother from the third planet to greet you.

This is the representative of the third planet. The numbers one, two and three do not indicate order in rank or location. We are all equal in every way, it is only that there has to be one following another in speaking. I, also greet our sister planet, Earth, and give you all my love and blessing. There is nothing to be added to that which has been said, so with good wishes for the advancement in understanding, love and joy of those inhabiting the planet Earth, I bid you dear ones farewell.

GLOSSARY OF FREQUENTLY USED SPACE TERMS

The following material has been excerpted from the Short Glossary of Space Terms, NASA publication SP-1. It includes words frequently appearing in popular space literature.

ablating material. A material designed to dissipate heat by vaporizing or melting.

Ablating materials are used on the surfaces of some reentry vehicles. Ablating materials absorb heat by increase in temperature and change in chemical or physical state. The heat is carried away from the surface by a loss of mass (liquid or vapor). The departing mass also blocks part of the convective heat transfer to the remaining material.

ablation. The removal of surface material from a body by vaporization, melting, or other process; specifically the intentional removal of material from a nose cone or spacecraft during high-speed movement through a planetary atmosphere used to provide thermal protection to the underlying structure. See ablating material.

abort. To cancel or cut short a flight.

absolute temperature. Temperature value relative to absolute zero.

absolute zero. The theoretical temperature at which all molecular motion ceases.

"Absolute zero" may be interpreted as the temperature at which the volume of a perfect gas vanishes, or more generally as the temperature of the cold source which would render a Carnot cycle 100 percent efficient. The value of absolute zero is now estimated to be −273.16° Celsius (Centigrade), −459.69° Fahrenheit, 0° Kelvin, and 0° Rankine.

acceleration. The rate of change of velocity.

Decrease in velocity is sometimes called "negative acceleration."

accelerometer. An instrument which measures acceleration or gravitational forces capable of imparting acceleration.

An accelerometer usually uses a concentrated mass (seismic mass) which resists movement because of its inertia. The displacement of the seismic mass relative to its supporting frame or container is used as a measure of acceleration.

acoustic velocity. The speed of propagation of sound waves. Also called "speed of sound."

acquisition. 1. The process of locating the orbit of a satellite or trajectory of a space probe so that tracking or telemetry data can be gathered. 2. The process of pointing an antenna or telescope so that it is properly oriented to allow gathering of tracking or telemetry data from a satellite or space probe.

acquisition and tracking radar. A radar set that locks onto a strong signal and tracks the object reflecting the signal.

active. Transmitting a signal, as "active satellite," in contrast to "passive."

adsorption. The adhesion of a thin film of liquid or gas to the surface of a solid substance. The solid does not combine chemically with the adsorbed substance.

aerobiology. The study of the distribution of living organisms freely suspended in the atmosphere.

aerodynamic heating. The heating of a body produced by passage of air or other gases over the body, significant chiefly at high speeds, caused by friction and by compression processes.

aerodynamics. The science that treats of the motion of air and other gaseous fluids, and of the forces acting on bodies when the bodies move through such fluids, or when such fluids move against or around the bodies, as "this research in aerodynamics."

aerodynamic vehicle. A device, such as an airplane, glider, etc., capable of flight only within a sensible atmosphere and relying on aerodynamic forces to maintain flight.

This term is used when the context calls for discrimination from "space vehicle."

aeroembolism. 1. The formation or liberation of gases in the blood vessels of the body, as brought on by a change from a high, or relatively high, atmospheric pressure to a lower one. 2. The disease or condition caused by the formation or liberation of gases in the body. The disease is characterized principally by neuralgic pains, cramps, and swelling, and sometimes results in death. Also called "decompression sickness."

aerolite. A meteorite composed principally of stony material.

aeronomy. The study of the upper regions of the atmosphere where physical and chemical reactions due to solar radiation take place.

aerospace. (From aeronautics and space.) Of or pertaining to both the earth's atmosphere and space, as in "aerospace industries."

aerospace medicine. That branch of medicine dealing with the effects of flight through the atmosphere or in space upon the human body, and with the prevention or cure of physiological or psychological malfunctions arising from these effects.

aerothermodynamic border. An altitude at about 100 miles, above which the atmosphere is so rarefied that the motion of an object through it at high speeds generates no significant surface heat.

aerothermodynamics. The study of the aerodynamic and thermodynamic problems connected with aerodynamic heating.

airglow. A relatively steady visible emission from the upper atmosphere, as distinguished from the sporadic emission of aurorae.

air sounding. The act of measuring atmospheric phenomena or determining atmospheric conditions at altitude, especially by means of apparatus carried by balloons or rockets.

albedo. The ratio of the amount of electromagnetic radiation reflected by a body to the amount falling upon it, commonly expressed as a percentage.

The term is used especially in reference to sunlight reflected from the moon or the planets.

alpha particle. A positively charged particle emitted from the nuclei of certain atoms during radioactive disintegration. The alpha particle has an atomic weight of 4 and a positive charge equal in magnitude to 2 electronic charges; hence it is essentially a helium nucleus.

ambient. Specifically, pertaining to the environment about a flying aircraft or other body but undisturbed or unaffected by it, as in "ambient air," or "ambient temperature."

analog computer. A computing machine that works on the principle of measuring, as distinguished from counting, in which the input data are made analogous to a measurement continuum, such as voltages, linear lengths, resistances, light intensities, etc., which can be manipulated by the computer.

Analog computers range from the relatively simple devices of the slide rule or airspeed indicator to complicated electrical machines used for solving mathematical problems.

angel. A radar echo caused by a physical phenomenon not discernible to the eye.

angstrom. A unit of length, used chiefly in expressing short wavelengths. Ten billion angstroms equal 1 meter.

annular eclipse. An eclipse in which a thin ring of the source of light appears around the obscuring body.

anoxia. A complete lack of oxygen available for physiological use within the body. Compare hypoxia.

"Anoxia" is popularly used as a synonym for "hypoxia." This usage should be avoided.

antigravity. A hypothetical effect that would arise from some energy field's cancellation of the effect of the gravitational field of the earth or other body.

aphelion. The point at which a planet or other celestial object in orbit about the sun is farthest from the sun.

apogee. In an orbit about the earth, the point at which the satellite is farthest from the earth; the highest altitude reached by a sounding rocket.

apogee rocket. A rocket attached to a satellite or spacecraft designed to fire when the craft is at apogee, the point farthest from the earth in orbit. The effect of the apogee rocket is to establish a new orbit farther from the earth or to allow the craft to escape from earth orbit.

arc-jet engine. A type of electrical rocket engine in which the propellant gas is heated by passing through an electric arc.

areo. Combining form of Ares (Mars) as in "areography."

Words with "areo" are considered pedantic by some, thus "geography of Mars" is preferred to "areography."

artificial gravity. A simulated gravity established within a space vehicle, as by rotating a cabin about an axis of a spacecraft, the centrifugal force generated being similar to the force of gravity.

asteroid. One of the many small celestial bodies revolving around the sun, most of the orbits being between those of Mars and Jupiter. Also called 'planetoid', 'minor planet'. See planet.

The term "minor planet" is preferred by many astronomers but "asteroid" continues to be used in astronomical literature, especially attributively, as in "asteroid belt."

astro. A prefix meaning "star" or "stars" and, by extension, sometimes used as the equivalent of "celestial," as in astronautics.

astroballistics. The study of the phenomena arising out of the motion of a solid through a gas at speeds high enough to cause ablation; for example, the interaction of a meteoroid with the atmosphere.

Astroballistics uses the data and methods of astronomy, aerodynamics, ballistics, and physical chemistry.

astrobiology. The study of living organisms on celestial bodies other than the earth.

astrodynamics. The practical application of celestial mechanics, astroballistics, propulsion theory, and allied fields to the problem of planning and directing the trajectories of space vehicles.

astronaut. 1. A person who occupies a space vehicle. 2. Specifically one of the test pilots selected to participate in Project Mercury, the first U.S. program for manned space flight.

astronautics. 1. The art, skill, or activity of operating space vehicles. 2. In a broader sense, the science of space flight.

astronomical unit. In the astronomical system of measures, a unit of length usually defined as the distance from the earth to the sun, approximately 92,900,000 statute miles or 149,600,000 kilometers.

atmosphere. The envelope of air surrounding the earth; also the body of gases surrounding or comprising any planet or other celestial body.

atomic clock. A precision clock that depends for its operation on an electrical oscillator (as a quartz crystal) regulated by the natural vibration frequencies of an atomic system (as a beam of cesium atoms or ammonia molecules).

attitude. The position or orientation of an aircraft, spacecraft, etc., either in motion or at rest, as determined by the relationship between its axes and some reference line or plane such as the horizon.

aurora. The sporadic visible emission from the upper atmosphere over middle and high latitudes. Also called "northern lights."

axis. (pl. axes) 1. A straight line about which a body rotates, or around which a plane figure may rotate to produce a solid; a line of symmetry. 2. One of a set of reference lines for certain systems of coordinates.

azimuth. Horizontal direction or bearing.

backup. 1. An item kept available to replace an item which fails to perform satisfactorily. 2. An item under development intended to perform the same general function performed by another item also under development.

Baker-Nunn camera. A large camera used in tracking satellites.

ballistics. The science that deals with the motion, behavior, and effects of projectiles, especially bullets, aerial bombs, rockets, or the like; the science or art of designing and hurling projectiles so as to achieve a desired performance.

ballistic trajectory. The trajectory followed by a body being acted upon only by gravitational forces and the resistance of the medium through which it passes.

A rocket without lifting surfaces is in a ballistic trajectory after its engines cease operating.

balloon-type rocket. A rocket, such as Atlas, that requires the pressure of its propellants (or other gases) within it to give it structural integrity.

beam. A ray or collection of focused rays of radiated energy. Radio waves used as a navigation aid.

beam-rider. A craft following a beam, particularly one which does so automatically, the beam providing the guidance.

binary notation. A system of positional notation in which the digits are coefficients of powers of the base 2 in the same way as the digits in the conventional decimal system are coefficients of powers of the base 10.

Binary notation employs only two digits, 1 and 0, therefore is used extensively in computers where the "on" and "off" positions of a switch or storage device can represent the two digits.

In decimal notation $111 = (1 \times 10^2) + (1 \times 10^1) + (1 \times 10^0) = 100 + 10 + 1 = $ *one hundred and eleven.*

In binary notation $111 = (1 \times 2^2) + (1 \times 2^1) + (1 \times 2^0) = 4 + 2 + 1 = $ *seven.*

bionics. The study of systems which function after the manner of, or in a manner characteristic of, or resembling, living systems.

bipropellant. A rocket propellant consisting of two unmixed or uncombined chemicals (fuel and oxidizer) fed to the combustion chamber separately.

bird. A colloquial term for a rocket, satellite, or spacecraft.

bit. (From binary digit.) A unit of information.

black box. Colloquially, any unit, usually an electronic device such as an amplifier, which can be mounted in a rocket, spacecraft, or the like as a single package.

blackout. 1. A fadeout of radio communications due to environmental factors such as ionospheric disturbances, or a plasma sheath surrounding a reentry vehicle. 2. A condition in which vision is temporarily obscured by a blackness, accompanied by a dullness of certain of the other senses, brought on by decreased blood pressure in the head and a consequent lack of oxygen, as may occur in pulling out of a high-speed dive in an airplane.

blip. See "pip."

blockhouse. (Also written "block house.") A reinforced-concrete structure, often built underground or partly underground, and sometimes dome-shaped, to provide protection against blast, heat, or explosion during rocket launchings or related activities; specifically, such a structure at a launch site that houses electronic control instruments used in launching a rocket.

boilerplate. As in "boilerplate capsule," a metal copy of the flight model, the structure or components of which are heavier than the flight model.

boiloff. The vaporization of a cold propellant such as liquid oxygen or liquid hydrogen, as the temperature of the propellant mass rises as in the tank of a rocket being readied for launch.

booster. Short for "booster engines" or "booster rocket."

booster engine. An engine, especially a booster rocket, that adds its thrust to the thrust of the sustainer engine.

booster rocket. 1. A rocket engine, either solid or liquid fuel, that assists the normal propulsive system or sustainer engine of a rocket or aeronautical vehicle by carrying the vehicle through some phase of its flight. 2. A rocket used to set a missile vehicle in motion before another engine takes over.

In sense 2 the term "launch vehicle" is more commonly used.

boostglide vehicle. A vehicle (half aircraft, half spacecraft) designed to fly to the limits of the sensible atmosphere, then be boosted by rockets into the space above, returning to earth by gliding under aerodynamic control.

braking ellipses. A series of ellipses, decreasing in size due to aerodynamic drag, followed by a spacecraft in entering a planetary atmosphere.

In theory, this maneuver will allow a spacecraft to dissipate energy through aerodynamic heating without burning up.

breakoff phenomenon. The feeling which sometimes occurs during high-altitude flight of being totally separated and detached from the earth and human society. Also called the "breakaway phenomenon."

burn. A period during which a rocket engine is firing, as in "second burn," the second period during a flight in which the engine is firing.

burnout. 1. An act or instance of the end of fuel and oxidizer burning in a rocket; the time at which this burnout occurs. Compare *cutoff*. 2. An act or instance of something burning out or of overheating; specifically, an act or instance of a rocket combustion chamber, nozzle, or other part overheating so as to result in damage or destruction.

capsule. 1. A boxlike component or unit, often sealed. 2. A small, sealed, pressurized cabin with an internal environment which will support life in a man or animal during extremely high altitude flight, space flight, or emergency escape.

celestial mechanics. The study of the theory of the motions of celestial bodies under the influence of gravitational fields.

celestial sphere. An imaginary sphere of infinite radius concentric with the earth, on which all celestial bodies except the earth are assumed to be projected.

centrifuge. Specifically, a large motor-driven apparatus with a long arm at the end of which human and animal subjects or equipment can be revolved and rotated at various speeds to simulate very closely the prolonged accelerations encountered in high-performance aircraft, rockets, and spacecraft.

chase pilot. A pilot who flies in an escort airplane advising a pilot who is making a check, training, or research flight in another craft.

checkout. A sequence of actions taken to test or examine a launch vehicle or spacecraft as to its readiness to perform its intended function.

chemical fuel. 1. A fuel that depends upon an oxidizer for combustion or for development of thrust, such as liquid or solid rocket fuel or internal-combustion engine fuel; distinguished from nuclear fuel. 2. A fuel that uses special chemicals, such as a boron-based fuel.

chemical rocket. A rocket using chemical fuel, fuel which requires an oxidizer for combustion, such as liquid or solid rocket fuel.

chemosphere. The vaguely defined region of the upper atmosphere in which photochemical reactions take place.

cislunar. (Latin *cis* "on this side.") Of or pertaining to phenomena, projects, or activity in the space between the earth and moon, or between the earth and the moon's orbit.

closed ecological system. A system that provides for the maintenance of life in an isolated living chamber such as a spacecraft cabin by means of a cycle wherein exhaled carbon dioxide, urine, and other waste matter are converted chemically or by photosynthesis into oxygen, water, and food.

coherent. Of electromagnetic radiation, being in phase so that waves at various points in space act in unison.

cold-flow test. A test of a liquid rocket without firing it to check or verify the efficiency of a propulsion subsystem, providing for the conditioning and flow of propellants (including tank pressurization, propellant loading, and propellant feeding).

comet. A luminous member of the solar system composed of a head or coma at the center of which a presumably solid nucleus is sometimes situated, and often with a spectacular gaseous tail extending a great distance from the head.

The orbits of comets are highly elliptical.

command. A signal which initiates or triggers an action in the device which receives the signal.

communications satellite. A satellite designed to reflect or relay radio or other communications waves.

companion body. A nose cone, last-stage rocket, or other body that orbits along with an earth satellite.

complex. Entire area of launch site facilities. This includes blockhouse, launch pad, gantry, etc. Also referred to as a "launch complex."

composite materials. Structural materials of metal alloys or plastics with built-in strengthening agents which may be in the form of filaments, foils, or flakes of a strong material.

composite propellant. A solid rocket propellant consisting of a fuel and an oxidizer.

computer. A machine for carrying out calculations and performing specified transformations on information.

configuration. A particular type of a specific aircraft, rocket, etc., which differs from others of the same model by virtue of the arrangement of its components or by the addition or omission of auxiliary equipment as "long-range configuration," "cargo configuration."

conic. A conic section.

conic section. A curve formed by the intersection of a plane and a right circular cone. Usually called "conic."

The conic sections are the ellipse, the parabola, and the hyperbola; curves that are used to describe the paths of bodies moving in space.

The circle is a special case of the ellipse, an ellipse with an eccentricity of zero.

console. An array of controls and indicators for the monitoring and control of a particular sequence of actions, as in the checkout of a rocket, a countdown action, or a launch procedure.

A console is usually designed around desklike arrays. It permits the operator to monitor and control different activating instruments, data recording instruments, or event sequencers.

control. Specifically, to direct the movements of an aircraft, rocket, or spacecraft with particular reference to changes in altitude and speed.

control rocket. A vernier engine, retrorocket, or other such rocket, used to guide or make small changes in the velocity of a rocket, spacecraft, or the like.

corona. The faintly luminous outer envelope of the sun. Also called "solar corona."

The corona can be observed at the earth's surface only at solar eclipse or with the coronagraph, a photographic instrument which artificially blocks out the image of the body of the sun.

cosmic dust. Small meteoroids of a size similar to dust.

cosmic rays. The extremely high energy subatomic particles which bombard the atmosphere from outer space. Cosmic-ray primaries seem to be mostly protons, hydrogen nuclei, but also comprise heavier nuclei. On colliding with atmospheric particles they produce many different kinds of lower-energy secondary cosmic radiation.

COSPAR. Abbreviation for "Committee on Space Research," International Council of Scientific Unions.

countdown. The time period in which a sequence of events is carried out to launch a rocket; the sequence of events.

cryogenic propellant. A rocket fuel, oxidizer, or propulsion fluid which is liquid only at very low temperatures.

cryogenic temperature. In general, a temperature range below about —50° C.; more particularly, temperatures within a few degrees of absolute zero.

cutoff. An act or instance of shutting something off; specifically in rocketry, an act or instance of shutting off the propellant flow in a rocket, or of stopping the combustion of the propellant.

data reduction. Transformation of observed values into useful, ordered, or simplified information.

deceleration. The act or process of moving, or of causing to move, with decreasing speed; the state of so moving.

deep space net. A combination of three radar and communications stations in the United States, Australia, and South Africa so located as to keep a spacecraft in deep space under observation at all times.

deep space probes. Spacecraft designed for exploring space to the vicinity of the moon and beyond. Deep space probes with specific missions may be referred to as "lunar probe," "Mars probe," "solar probe," etc.

destruct. The deliberate action of destroying a rocket vehicle after it has been launched, but before it has completed its course.

Destructs are executed when the rocket gets off its plotted course or functions in a way so as to become a hazard.

digital computer. A computer which operates on the principle of counting as opposed to measuring. See **analog computer.**

diplexer. A device permitting an antenna system to be used simultaneously or separately by two transmitters. Compare with **duplexer.**

dish. A parabolic type of radio or radar antenna, roughly the shape of a soup bowl.

display. The graphic presentation of the output data of a device or system as, for example a radarscope.

docking. The process of bringing two spacecraft together while in space.

Doppler shift. The change in frequency with which energy reaches a receiver when the source of radiation or a reflector of the radiation and the receiver are in motion relative to each other. The Doppler shift is used in many tracking and navigation systems.

dosimeter. A device, worn by persons working around radioactive material, which indicates the amount (dose) of radiation to which they have been exposed.

Dovap. From _D_oppler, _v_elocity and _p_osition, a tracking system which uses the Doppler shift caused by a target moving relative to a ground transmitter to obtain velocity and position information.

drogue parachute. A type of parachute attached to a body, used to slow it down; also called "deceleration parachute," or "drag parachute."

duplexer. A device which permits a single antenna system to be used for both transmitting and receiving.

"Duplexer" should not be confused with "diplexer," a device permitting an antenna system to be used simultaneously or separately by two transmitters.

dynamic pressure. (Symbol q.) 1. The pressure exerted by a fluid, such as air, by virtue of its motion. 2. The pressure exerted on a body, by virtue of its motion through a fluid, for example, the pressure exerted on a rocket moving through the atmosphere.

eccentric. Not having the same center; varying from a circle, as in "eccentric orbit."

ecliptic. The apparent annual path of the sun among the stars; the intersection of the plane of the earth's orbit with the celestial sphere.

This is a great circle of the celestial sphere inclined at an angle of about 23°27' to the celestial equator.

ecological system. A habitable environment, either created artificially, such as in a manned space vehicle, or occurring naturally, such as the environment on the surface of the earth, in which man, animals, or other organisms can live in mutual relationship with each other.

Ideally, the environment furnishes the sustenance for life, and the resulting waste products revert or cycle back into the environment to be used again for the continuous support of life.

ejection capsule. 1. In an aircraft or manned spacecraft, a detachable compartment serving as a cockpit or cabin, which may be rejected as a unit and parachuted to the ground. 2. In an artificial satellite, probe, or unmanned spacecraft, a boxlike unit usually containing recording instruments or records of observed data, which may be ejected and returned to earth by a parachute or other deceleration device.

electric propulsion. The generation of thrust from a rocket engine involving acceleration of a propellant by some electrical device such as an arc jet, ion engine, or magnetohydrodynamic accelerator.

electromagnetic radiation. Energy propagated through space or through material media in the form of an advancing disturbance in electrical and magnetic fields existing in space or in the media. Also called simply "radiation."

electron. The subatomic particle that possesses the smallest possible electric charge.

The term "electron" is usually reserved for the orbital particle whereas the term "beta particle" refers to a particle of the same electric charge inside the nucleus of the atom.

electronic data processing. The use of electronic devices and systems in the processing of data so as to interpret the data and put it into usable form.

ellipse. A plane curve constituting the locus of all points the sum of whose distances from two fixed points called "loci" is constant; an elongated circle. See conic section.

The orbits of planets, satellites, planetoids, and comets are ellipses; center of attraction is at one focus.

environment. An external condition or the sum of such conditions, in which a piece of equipment or a system operates, as in "temperature environment," "vibration environment," or "space environment."

Environments are usually specified by a range of values, and may be either natural or artificial.

epoch. A particular instant for which certain data are valid.

escape velocity. The radial speed which a particle or larger body must attain in order to escape from the gravitational field of a planet or star.

The escape velocity from Earth is approximately 7 miles per sec.; from Mars, 3.2 miles per sec.; and from the Sun, 390 miles per sec. In order for a celestial body to retain an atmosphere for astronomically long periods of time, the mean velocity of the atmospheric molecules must be considerably below the escape velocity.

exobiology. The study of living organisms existing on celestial bodies other than the earth.

exosphere. The outermost, or topmost portion of the atmosphere.

In the exosphere, the air density is so low that the mean free path of individual particles depends upon their direction with respect to the local vertical, being greatest for upward moving particles. It is only from the exosphere that atmospheric gases can, to any appreciable extent, escape into outer space.

exotic fuel. Any fuel considered to be unusual, as a boron-based fuel.

explosive bolt. A bolt incorporating an explosive which can be detonated on command, thus destroying the bolt. Explosive bolts are used, for example, in separating a satellite from a rocket.

extraterrestrial. From outside the earth.

eyeballs in, eyeballs out. Terminology used by test pilots to describe the acceleration experienced by the person being accelerated. Thus the acceleration experienced by an astronaut at liftoff is "eyeballs in" positive g in terms of vehicle acceleration), and the acceleration experienced when retrorockets fire is "eyeballs out" (negative g in terms of vehicle acceleration).

fallaway section. A section of a rocket vehicle that is cast off and separates from the vehicle during flight, especially such a section that falls back to the earth.

fatigue. A weakening or deterioration of metal or other material, or of a member, occurring under load, especially under repeated, cyclic, or continued loading.

field. A region of space at each point of which a given physical quantity has some definite value, thus a "gravitational field," an "electric field," a "magnetic field," etc.

film cooling. The cooling of a body or surface, such as the inner surface of a rocket combustion chamber, by maintaining a thin fluid layer over the affected area.

fixed satellite. An earth satellite that orbits from west to east at such a speed as to remain constantly over a given place on the earth's equator.

flare. A bright eruption from the sun's chromosphere.

Flares may appear within minutes and fade within an hour. They cover a wide range of intensity and size, and they tend to occur between sunspots.

Flares are related to radio fadeouts and terrestrial magnetic disturbances.

flashback. A reversal of flame propagation in a system, counter to the usual flow of the combustible mixture.

flux. The rate of flow of some quantity, often used in reference to the flow of some form of energy.

flying test bed. An aircraft, rocket, or other flying vehicle used to carry objects or devices being flight tested.

free fall. 1. The fall or drop of a body, such as a rocket, not guided, not under thrust, and not retarded by a parachute or other braking device. 2. Weightlessness.

g or G. An acceleration equal to the acceleration of gravity, approximately 32.2 feet per second per second at sea level; used as a unit of stress measurement for bodies undergoing acceleration.

gamma ray. An electromagnetic radiation of wave form emitted by a radioactive nucleus and similar to X-rays but of higher energy and shorter wavelength.

gantry. A frame structure that spans over something, as an elevated platform that runs astride a work area, supported by wheels on each side; specifically, short for "gantry crane" or "gantry scaffold."

gantry scaffold. A massive scaffolding structure mounted on a bridge or platform supported by a pair of towers or trestles that normally run back and forth on parallel tracks, used to assemble and service a large rocket on its launching pad. Often shortened to "gantry." Also called "service tower."

This structure is a latticed arrangement of girders, tubing, platforms, cranes, elevators, instruments, wiring, floodlights, cables, and ladders—all used to attend the rocket.

garbage. Miscellaneous objects in orbit, usually material ejected or broken away from a launch vehicle or satellite.

gas cap. The gas immediately in front of a meteoroid or reentry body as it travels through the atmosphere; the leading portion of a meteor. This gas is compressed and adiabatically heated to incandescence.

generation. In any technical or technological development, as of a missile, jet engine, or the like, a stage or period that is marked by features or performances not marked, or existent, in a previous period of development or production, as in "second generation rocket."

geo. A prefix meaning "earth," as in "geology," "geophysics."

Most writers use the established terms such as "geology" to refer to the same concept on other bodies of the solar system, as "the geology of Mars," rather than "mareology," or "marsology," "geology of the moon," rather than "selenology."

geocentric. Relative to the earth as a center; measured from the center of the earth.

geodetic. Pertaining to geodesy, the science which deals with the size and shape of the earth.

geomagnetism. The magnetic phenomena, collectively considered, exhibited by the earth and its atmosphere; by extension, the magnetic phenomena in interplanetary space.

geophysics. The physics of the earth and its environment, i.e., earth, air, and (by extension) space.

Classically, geophysics is concerned with the nature of physical occurrences at and below the surface of the earth including, therefore, geology, oceanography, geodesy, seismology, hydrology, etc. The trend is to extend the scope of geophysics to include meteorology, geomagnetism, astrophysics, and other sciences concerned with the physical nature of the universe.

geoprobe. A rocket vehicle designed to explore space near the earth at a distance of more than 4,000 miles from the earth's surface. Rocket vehicles operating lower than 4,000 miles are termed "sounding rockets."

giga. A prefix meaning multiplied by 1 billion.

gimbal. 1. A device with two mutually perpendicular and intersecting axes of rotation, thus giving free angular movement in two directions, on which an engine or other object may be mounted. 2. In a gyro, a support which provides the spin axis with a degree of freedom.

gnotobiotics. The study of germ free animals.

gravitation. The acceleration produced by the mutual attraction of two masses, directed along the line joining their centers of mass, and of magnitude inversely proportional to the square of the distance between the two centers of mass.

gravity. The force imparted by the earth to a mass on, or close to the earth. Since the earth is rotating, the force observed as gravity is the resultant of the force of gravitation and the centrifugal force arising from this rotation.

g-suit or G-suit. A suit that exerts pressure on the abdomen and lower parts of the body to prevent or retard the collection of blood below the chest under positive acceleration.

g-tolerance. A tolerance in a person or other animal, or in a piece of equipment, to an acceleration of a particular value.

guidance. The process of directing the movements of an aeronautical vehicle or space vehicle, with particular reference to the selection of a flight path or trajectory.

gyro. A device which utilizes the angular momentum of a spinning rotor to sense angular motion of its base about one or two axes at right angles to the spin axis. Also called "gyroscope."

hardness. Of X-rays and other radiation. Radiation energy, a measure of penetrating power. Radiation which will penetrate a 10-centimeter thickness of lead is considered "hard radiation."

heat exchanger. A device for transferring heat from one fluid to another without intermixing the fluids.

heat shield. Any device that protects something from heat.

heat sink. A material capable of absorbing heat; a device utilizing such a material and used as a thermal protection device on a spacecraft or reentry vehicle.

hold. During a countdown: To halt the sequence of events until an impediment has been removed so that the countdown can be resumed, as in "T minus 40 and holding."

hot test. A propulsion system test conducted by actually firing the propellants.

human engineering. The art or science of designing, building, or equipping mechanical devices or artificial environments to the anthropometric, physiological, or psychological requirements of the men who will use them.

hypersonic. 1. Pertaining to hypersonic flow. 2. Pertaining to speeds of Mach 5 or greater.

hypersonic flow. In aerodynamics, flow of a fluid over a body at speeds much greater than the speed of sound and in which the shock waves start at a finite distance from the surface of the body.

hypoxia. Oxygen deficiency in the blood, cells, or tissues of the body in such degree as to cause psychological and physiological disturbances.

Hypoxia may result from a scarcity of oxygen in the air being breathed, or from an inability of the body tissues to absorb oxygen under conditions of low ambient pressure. In the latter case, water vapors from body fluids increase in the sacs of the lungs, crowding out the oxygen.

igniter. Any device used to begin combustion, such as a spark plug in the combustion chamber of a jet engine, or a squib used to ignite fuel in a rocket.

impact area. The area in which a rocket strikes the earth's surface.

Used specifically in reference to the "impact area" of a rocket range.

impact bag. An inflatable bag attached to a spacecraft or reentry capsule to absorb part of the shock of landing.

inertial guidance. Guidance by means of acceleration measured and integrated within the craft.

infrared. Infrared radiation; electromagnetic radiation in the wavelength interval from the red end of the visible spectrum on the lower limit to microwaves used in radar on the upper limit.

insertion. The process of putting an artificial satellite into orbit. Also the time of such action.

interferometer. An apparatus used to produce and measure interference from two or more coherent wave trains from the same source.

Interferometers are used to measure wavelengths, to measure angular width of sources, to determine the angular position of sources (as in satellite tracking), and for many other purposes.

ion. An atom or molecularly bound group of atoms having an electric charge. Sometimes also a free electron or other charged subatomic particle.

ionosphere. The part of the earth's outer atmosphere where ions and electrons are present in quantities sufficient to affect the propagation of radio waves.

Kepler's laws. The three empirical laws describing the motions of planets in their orbits, discovered by Johannes Kepler (1571–1630). These are: (1) The orbits of the planets are ellipses, with the sun at a common focus. (2) As a planet moves in its orbit, the line joining the planet and sun sweeps over equal areas in equal intervals of time. Also called "law of equal areas." (3) The squares of the periods of revolution of any two planets are proportional to the cubes of their mean distances from the sun.

laser. (From *light amplification by stimulated emission of radiation*). A device for producing light by emission of energy stored in a molecular or atomic system when stimulated by an input signal.

launch pad. The load-bearing base or platform from which a rocket vehicle is launched. Usually called "pad."

launch ring. The metal ring on the launch pad on which a missile stands before launch.

launch vehicle. Any device which propels and guides a spacecraft into orbit about the earth or into a trajectory to another celestial body. Often called "booster."

launch window. An interval of time during which a rocket can be launched to accomplish a particular purpose as "liftoff occurred 5 minutes after the beginning of the 82-minute launch window."

liberation. A real or apparent oscillatory motion, particularly the apparent oscillation of the moon.

Because of liberation, more than half of the moon's surface is revealed to an observer on the earth, even though the same side of the moon is always toward the earth because the moon's periods of rotation and revolution are the same.

liftoff. The action of a rocket vehicle as it separates from its launch pad in a vertical ascent.

A liftoff is applicable only to vertical ascent; a takeoff is applicable to ascent at any angle. A liftoff is action performed by a rocket; a launch is action performed upon a rocket or upon a satellite or spaceship carried by a rocket.

liquid-propellant rocket engine. A rocket engine fueled with a propellant or propellants in liquid form. Also called "liquid-propellant rocket."

Rocket engines of this kind vary somewhat in complexity, but they consist essentially of one or more combustion chambers together with the necessary pipes, valves, pumps, injectors, etc.

longitudinal axis. The fore-and-aft line through the center of gravity of a craft.

lox. 1. Liquid oxygen. Used attributively as in "lox tank," "lox unit." Also called "loxygen." 2. To load the fuel tanks of a rocket vehicle with liquid oxygen. Hence, "loxing."

Mach number. (After Ernst Mach (1838–1916), Austrian scientist.) A number expressing the ratio of the speed of a body or of a point on a body with respect to the surrounding air or other fluid, or the speed of a flow, to the speed of sound in the medium; the speed represented by this number.

If the Mach number is less than one, the flow is called "subsonic" and local disturbances can propagate ahead of the flow. If the Mach number is greater than one, the flow is called "supersonic" and disturbance cannot propagate ahead of the flow, with the result that shock waves form.

magnetic storm. A worldwide disturbance of the earth's magnetic field.

Magnetic storms are frequently characterized by a sudden onset, in which the magnetic field undergoes marked changes in the course of an hour or less, followed by a very gradual return to normality, which may take several days. Magnetic storms are caused by solar disturbances, though the exact nature of the link between the solar and terrestrial disturbances is not understood. Sometimes a magnetic storm can be linked to a particular solar disturbance. In these cases, the time between solar flare and onset of the magnetic storm is about 1 or 2 days, suggesting that the disturbance is carried to the earth by a cloud of particles thrown out by the sun.

magnetohydrodynamics. The study of the interaction that exists between a magnetic field and an electrically conducting fluid. Also called "magnetoplasmadynamics," "magnetogasdynamics," "hydromagnetics," "MHD."

magnetometer. An instrument used in the study of geomagnetism for measuring any magnetic element.

magnitude. Relative brightness of a celestial body. The smaller the magnitude number, the brighter the body.

Decrease of light by a factor of 100 increases the stellar magnitude by 5.00; hence the brightest objects have negative magnitudes. (Sun: -26.8; mean full moon: -12.5; Venus at brightest: -4.3; Jupiter at opposition: -2.3; Sirius: -1.6; Vega: $+0.2$; Polaris: $+2.1$). The faintest stars visible to the naked eye on a clear dark night are of about the sixth magnitude.

main stage. 1. In a multistage rocket, the stage that develops the greatest amount of thrust, with or without booster engines. 2. In a single-stage rocket vehicle powered by one or more engines, the period when full thrust (at or above 90 percent) is attained. 3. A sustainer engine, considered as a stage after booster engines have fallen away, as in the main stage of the Atlas.

manometer. An instrument for measuring pressure of gases and vapors both above and below atmospheric pressure.

maser. An amplifier utilizing the principle of *microwave amplification by stimulated emission of radiation*. Emission of energy stored in a molecular or atomic system by a microwave power supply is stimulated by the input signal.

mass. The measure of the amount of matter in a body, thus its inertia.

The weight of a body is the force with which it is attracted by the earth.

mass-energy equivalence. The equivalence of a quantity of mass m and a quantity of energy E, the two quantities being related by the mass-energy relation $E = mc^2$, where $c =$ the speed of light.

mass ratio. The ratio of the mass of the propellant charge of a rocket to the total mass of the rocket charged with the propellant.

mate. To fit together two major components of a system.

mega. A prefix meaning multiplied by 1 million as in "megacycles."

memory. The component of a computer, control system, guidance system, instrumented satellite, or the like designed to provide ready access to data or instructions previously recorded so as to make them bear upon an immediate problem, such as the guidance of a physical object, or the analysis and reduction of data.

meteor. In particular, the light phenomenon which results from the entry into the earth's atmosphere of a solid particle from space: more generally, any physical object or phenomenon associated with such an event.

meteoric. Of or pertaining to meteors, or meteoroids.

meteorite. A meteoroid which has reached the surface of the earth without being completely vaporized.

meteoroid. A solid object moving in interplanetary space, of a size considerably smaller than an asteroid and considerably larger than an atom or molecule.

meteorological rocket. A rocket designed primarily for routine upper-air observation (as opposed to research) in the lower 250,000 feet of the atmosphere, especially that portion inaccessible to baloons; i.e., above 100,000 feet. Also called "rocketsonde."

micro. 1. A prefix meaning divided by 1 million. 2. A prefix meaning very small as in "micrometeorite."

micrometeoroid. A very small meteoroid or meteoric particle with a diameter in general of less than a millimeter.

microwave region. Commonly that region of the radio spectrum between approximately 1,000 megacycles and 300,000 megacycles.

mini. A contraction of "miniature" used in combination, as in "minicomponent," "miniradio," "minitransistor."

miniaturize. To construct a functioning miniature of a part or instrument. Said of telemetering instruments or parts used in an earth satellite or rocket vehicle, where room is at a premium. Hence "miniaturized," "miniaturization."

missile. Any object thrown, dropped, fired, launched, or otherwise projected with the purpose of striking a target. Short for "ballistic missile," "guided missile."

Missile is loosely used as a synonym for "rocket" or "spacecraft" by some careless writers.

mockup. A full-sized replica or dummy of something, such as a spacecraft, often made of some substitute material, such as wood and sometimes incorporating functioning pieces of equipment, such as engines.

modulation. Specifically, variation of some characteristic of a radio wave, called the "carrier wave," in accordance with instantaneous values of another wave, called the "modulating wave."

Variation of amplitude is amplitude modulation, variation of frequency is frequency modulation, and variation of phase is phase modulation. The formation of very short bursts of a carrier wave, separated by relatively long periods during which no carrier wave is transmitted, is pulse modulation.

module. 1. A self-contained unit of a launch vehicle or spacecraft which serves as a building block for the overall structure. The module is usually designated by its primary function as "command module," "lunar landing module," etc. 2. A one-package assembly of functionally associated electronic parts; usually a plug-in unit.

molecule. An aggregate of two or more atoms of a substance that exists as a unit.

monopropellant. A rocket propellant consisting of a single substance, especially a liquid, capable of producing a heated jet without the addition of a second substance.

multiplexer. A mechanical or electrical device for sharing of a circuit by two or more coincident signals.

multiplexing. The simultaneous transmission of two or more signals within single channel.

The three basic methods of multiplexing involve the separation of signals by time division, frequency division, and phase division.

multipropellant. A rocket propellant consisting of two or more substances fed separately to the combustion chamber.

multistage rocket. A vehicle having two or more rocket units, each unit firing after the one in back of it has exhausted its propellant. Normally, each unit, or stage, is jettisoned after completing its firing. Also called a "multiple-stage rocket" or, infrequently, a "step rocket."

nano. A prefix meaning divided by 1 billion, as in "nanosecond," one-billionth of a second.

neutron. A subatomic particle with no electric charge, having a mass slightly more than the mass of the proton.

Newton's laws of motion. A set of three fundamental postulates forming the basis of the mechanics of rigid bodies, formulated by Newton in 1687.

The first law is concerned with the principle of inertia and states that if a body in motion is not acted upon by an external force, its momentum remains constant (law of conservation of momentum). The second law asserts that the rate of change of momentum of a body is proportional to the force acting upon the body and is in the direction of the applied force. A familiar statement of this is the equation

$$F = ma,$$

Where F is vector sum of the applied forces, m the mass, and a the vector acceleration of the body. The third law is the principle of action and reaction, stating that for every force acting upon a body there exists a corresponding force of the same magnitude exerted by the body in the opposite direction.

noise. Any undesired sound. By extension, noise is any unwanted disturbance within a useful frequency band, such as undesired electric waves in a transmission channel or device. When caused by natural electrical discharges in the atmosphere noise may be called "static."

normal shock wave. A shock wave perpendicular, or substantially so, to the direction of flow in a supersonic flow field. Sometimes shortened to "normal shock."

nosecone. The cone-shaped leading end of a rocket vehicle, consisting of (a) of a chamber or chambers in which a satellite, instruments, animals, plants, or auxiliary equipment may be carried, and (b) of an outer surface built to withstand high temperatures generated by aerodynamic heating.

In a satellite vehicle, the nosecone may become the satellite itself after separating from the final stage of the rocket or it may be used to shield the satellite until orbital speed is accomplished, then separating from the satellite.

nova. A star which suddenly becomes many times brighter than previously, and then gradually fades.

nozzle. Specifically, the part of a rocket thrust chamber assembly in which the gases produced in the chamber are accelerated to high velocities.

nuclear fuel. Fissionable material of reasonably long life, used or usable in producing energy in a nuclear reactor.

nuclear radiation. The emission of neutrons and other particles from an atomic nucleus as the result of nuclear fission or nuclear fusion.

nuclear reactor. An apparatus in which nuclear fission may be sustained in a self-supporting chain reaction. Commonly called "reactor."

nucleus. The positively charged core of an atom with which is associated practically the whole mass of the atom but only a minute part of its volume.

A nucleus is composed of one or more protons and an approximately equal number of neutrons.

occultation. The disappearance of a body behind another body of larger apparent size.

When the moon passes between the observer and a star, the star is said to be occulted.

octave. The interval between any two frequencies having the ratio of 1:2.

orbit. 1. The path of a body or particle under the influence of a gravitational or other force. For instance, the orbit of a celestial body is its path relative to another body around which it revolves. 2. To go around the earth or other body in an orbit.

orbital elements. A set of 7 parameters defining the orbit of a satellite.

orbital period. The interval between successive passages of a satellite.

orbital velocity. 1. The average velocity at which an earth satellite or other orbiting body travels around its primary. 2. The velocity of such a body at any given point in its orbit, as in "its orbital velocity at the apogee is less than at the perigee."

order of magnitude. A factor of 10.

Two quantities of the same kind which differ by less than a factor of 10 are said to be of the same order of magnitude. "Order of magnitude" is used loosely by many writers to mean a pronounced difference in quantity but with the difference much less or much more than a factor of 10.

oxidizer. Specifically, a substance (not necessarily containing oxygen) that supports the combustion of a fuel or propellant.

pad. The platform from which a rocket vehicle is launched. See "launch pad."

paraglider. A flexible-winged, kite-like vehicle designed for use in a recovery system for launch vehicles or as a reentry vehicle.

passive. Reflecting a signal without transmission, as "Echo is a passive satellite." Contrasted with "active."

payload. 1. Originally, the revenue-producing portion of an aircraft's load, e.g., passengers, cargo, mail, etc. 2. By extension, that which an aircraft, rocket, or the like carries over and above what is necessary for the operation of the vehicle during its flight.

peri. A prefix meaning near, as in "perigee."

perigee. That orbital point nearest the earth when the earth is the center of attraction.

That orbital point farthest from the earth is called "apogee." Perigee and apogee are used by many writers in referring to orbits of satellites, especially artificial satellites, around any planet or satellite, thus avoiding coinage of new terms for each planet and moon.

perturbation. Specifically, a disturbance in the regular motion of a celestial body, the result of a force additional to those which cause the regular motion.

photon. According to the quantum theory of radiation, the elementary quantity, or "quantum," of radiant energy.

photon engine. A projected type of reaction engine in which thrust would be obtained from a stream of electromagnetic radiation.

Although the thrust of this engine would be minute, it may be possible to apply it for extended periods of time. Theoretically, in space, where no resistance is offered by air particles, very high speeds may be built up.

photosphere. The intensely bright portion of the sun visible to the unaided eye.

physiological acceleration. The acceleration experienced by a human or an animal test subject in an accelerating vehicle.

pickoff. A sensing device, used in combination with a gyroscope in an automatic pilot or other automatic or robot apparatus, that responds to angular movement to create a signal or to effect some type of control.

pickup. A device that converts a sound, view, or other form of intelligence into corresponding electric signals (e.g. a microphone, a television camera, or a phonograph pickup).

pico. A prefix mening divided by 1 million million.

pip. Signal indication on the scope of an electronic instrument, produced by a short, sharply peaked pulse of voltage. Also called "blip."

pitchover. The programed turn from the vertical that a rocket under power takes as it describes an arc and points in a direction other than vertical.

planet. A celestial body of the solar system, revolving around the sun in a nearly circular orbit, or a similar body revolving around a star.

The larger of such bodies are sometimes called "principal planets" to distinguish them from asteroids, planetoids, or minor planets, which are comparatively very small.

An inferior planet has an orbit smaller than that of the earth; a superior planet has an orbit larger than that of the earth. The four planets nearest the sun are called "inner planets"; the others, "outer planets." The four largest planets are called "major planets." The word "planet" is of Greek origin meaning, literally, wanderer, applied because the planets appear to move relative to the stars.

plasma. An electrically conductive gas comprised of neutral particles, ionized particles, and free electrons but which, taken as a whole, is electrically neutral.

plasma engine. A reaction engine using magnetically accelerated plasma as propellant.

A plasma engine is a type of electrical engine.

plasma jet. A magnetohydrodynamic rocket engine in which the ejection of plasma generates thrust.

plasma sheath. An envelope of ionized gas that surrounds a body moving through an atmosphere at hypersonic velocities.

The plasma sheath affects transmission, reception, and diffraction of radio waves, thus is important in operational problems of spacecraft.

polarization. A state of electromagnetic radiation in which transverse vibrations take place in some regular manner; e.g., all in one plane, in a circle, in an ellipse, or in some other definite curve.

posigrade rocket. An auxiliary rocket which fires in the direction in which the vehicle is pointed, used for example in separating two stages of a vehicle.

precession. The change in the direction of the axis of rotation of a spinning body or of the plane of the orbit of an orbiting body when acted upon by an outside force.

pressure suit. A garment designed to provide the human body an environment above ambient pressure so that respiratory and circulatory functions may continue normally, or nearly so, under low-pressure conditions, such as occur at high altitudes or in space without benefit of a pressurized cabin.

pressurized. Containing air, or other gas, at a pressure that is higher than the pressure outside the container.

prestage. A step in the action of igniting a large liquid rocket taken prior to the ignition of the full flow, and consisting of igniting a partial flow of propellants into the thrust chamber.

primary. 1. Short for "primary body." 2. Short for "primary cosmic ray."

primary body. The spatial body about which a satellite or other body orbits, or from which it is escaping, or towards which it is falling.

The primary body of the moon is the earth; the primary body of the earth is the sun.

primary cosmic rays. High-energy particles originating outside the earth's atmosphere.

Primary cosmic rays appear to come from all directions in space.

probe. Any device inserted in an environment for the purpose of obtaining information about the environment, specifically, an instrumented vehicle moving through the upper atmosphere or space, or landing upon another celestial body in order to obtain information about the specific environment.

prominence. A filament-like protuberance from the visible portion of the sun.

propellant. Short for "rocket propellant."

proton. A positively charged subatomic particle of a positive charge equal to the negative charge of the electron but of 1,837 times the mass; a constituent of all atomic nuclei.

proving stand. A test stand for reaction engines, especially rocket engines.

purge. To rid a line or tank of residual fluid, especially of fuel or oxygen in the tanks or lines of a rocket after a test firing or simulated test firing.

quantum theory. The theory (first stated by Max Planck before the Physical Society of Berlin on December 14, 1900) that all electromagnetic radiation is emitted and absorbed in "quanta" each of magnitude $h\nu$, h being Planck's constant and ν the frequency of the radiation.

radar astronomy. The study of celestial bodies within the solar system by means of radiation originating on earth but reflected from the body under observation. See radio astronomy.

radiation. Short for "electromagnetic radiation," "nuclear radiation."

radiation pressure. Pressure exerted upon a body by electromagnetic radiation incident upon body.

radiation shield. 1. A device used on certain types of instruments to prevent unwanted radiation from biasing the measurement of a quantity. 2. A device used to protect bodies from the harmful effects of nuclear radiation, cosmic radiation, or the like.

radiator. 1. Any source of radiant energy, especially electromagnetic radiation. 2. A device that dissipates heat from something, as from water or oil, not necessarily by radiation only.

Generally, the application of the terms "radiator" (in sense 2) or "heat exchanger" to a particular apparatus depends upon the point of view: If the emphasis is upon merely getting rid of heat, "radiator" is most often used, or sometimes "cooler;" if the emphasis is upon transferring heat, "heat exchanger" is used—but these distinctions do not always hold true.

radio astronomy. The study of celestial objects through observation of radiofrequency waves emitted or reflected by these objects.

radio meteor. A meteor detected by the reflection of a radio signal from the meteor trail of relatively high ion density (ion column).

Such an ion column is left behind a meteoroid when it reaches the region of the upper atmosphere between about 80 and 120 km, although occasionally radio meteors are detected at higher altitudes.

radiosonde. A balloon-borne instrument for the simultaneous measurement and transmission of meteorological data.

radio telescope. A device for receiving, amplifying, and measuring the intensity of radio waves originating outside the earth's atmosphere.

reaction control system. A system of controlling the attitude of a craft when outside the atmosphere by using jets of gas in lieu of aerodynamic control surfaces.

reaction engine. An engine that develops thrust by its reaction to ejection of a substance from it; specifically, such an engine that ejects a jet or stream of gases created by the burning of fuel within the engine.

A reaction engine operates in accordance with Newton's third law of motion; i.e., to every action (force) there is an equal and opposite reaction. Both rocket engines and jet engines are reaction engines.

readout. The action of a radio transmitter transmitting data either instantaneously with the acquisition of the data or by play of a magnetic tape upon which the data have been recorded.

readout station. A recording or receiving ratio station at which data are received from a transmitter in a probe, satellite, or other spacecraft.

real time. Time in which reporting on events or recording of events is simultaneous with the events.

For example, the real time of a satellite is that time in which it simultaneously reports its environment as it encounters it; the real time of a computer is that time during which it is accepting data.

recombination. The process by which a positive and a negative ion join to form a neutral molecule or other neutral particle.

recovery. The procedure or action that obtains when the whole of a satellite, or a section, instrumentation package, or other part of a rocket vehicle is recovered after a launch; the result of this procedure.

recycle. In a countdown: To stop the count and to return to an earlier point in the countdown, as in "we have recycled, now at T minus 80 and counting." Compare hold.

red shift. In astronomy, the displacement of observed spectral lines toward the longer wavelengths of the red end of the spectrum. Compare space reddening.

The "red shift" in the spectrum of distant galaxies has been interpreted as evidence that the universe is expanding.

reentry. The event occurring when a spacecraft or other object comes back into the sensible atmosphere after being rocketed to altitudes above the sensible atmosphere; the action involved in this event.

reentry vehicle. A space vehicle designed to return with its payload to earth through the sensible atmosphere.

reentry window. The area at the limits of the earth's atmosphere through which a spacecraft in a given trajectory can pass to accomplish a successful reentry.

regenerative cooling. The cooling of a part of an engine by the propellant being delivered to the combustion chamber; specifically, the cooling of a rocket-engine combustion chamber or nozzle by circulating the fuel or oxidizer, or both, around the part to be cooled.

regenerator. A device used in a therodynamic process for capturing and returning to the process heat that would otherwise be lost.

relativistic. In general, pertaining to material, as a subatomic particle, moving at speeds which are an appreciable fraction of the speed of light.

relativity. A principle that postulates the equivalence of the description of the universe, in terms of physical laws, by various observers, or for various frames of reference.

rendezvous. The event of two or more objects meeting at a preconceived time and place.

A rendezvous would be involved, for example, in servicing or resupplying a space station.

retrorocket. (From "retroacting.") A rocket fitted on or in a spacecraft, satellite, or the like to produce thrust opposed to forward motion.

revolution. Motion of a celestial body in its orbit; circular motion about an axis usually external to the body.

In some contexts the terms "revolution" and "rotation" are used interchangeably; but with reference to the motions of a celestial body, "revolution" refers to the motion in an orbit or about an axis external to the body, while "rotation" refers to motion about an axis within the body. Thus, the earth revolves about the sun annually and rotates about its axis daily.

rocket. 1. A projectile, pyrotechnic device, or flying vehicle propelled by a rocket engine. 2. A rocket engine.

rocket engine. A reaction engine that contains within itself, or carries along with itself, all the substances necessary for its operation or for the consumption or combustion of its fuel, not requiring intake of any outside substance and hence capable of operation in outer space. Also called "rocket motor."

rocket propellant. Any agent used for consumption or combustion in a rocket and from which the rocket derives its thrust, such as a fuel, oxidizer, additive, catalyst, or any compound or mixture of these. "Rocket propellant" is often shortened to "propellant."

rocketsonde. Meterological rocket.

rockoon. A high-altitude sounding system consisting of a small solid-propellant research rocket launched from a large plastic balloon.

The rocket is fired near the maximum altitude of the balloon flight. It is a relatively mobile rocket-sounding system, and has been used extensively from shipboard.

roll. The rotational or oscillatory movement of an aircraft or similar body which takes place about a longitudinal axis through the body—called "roll" for any amount of such rotation.

rotation. Turning of a body about an axis within the body, as the daily rotation of the earth. See revolution.

rumble. A form of combustion instability, especially in a liquid-propellant rocket engine, characterized by a low-pitched, low-frequency rumbling noise; the noise made in this kind of combustion.

satellite. 1. An attendant body that revolves about another body, the primary; especially in the solar system, a secondary body, or moon, that revolves about a planet. 2. A manmade object that revolves about a spatial body, such as Explorer I orbiting about the earth.

scrub. To cancel a scheduled rocket firing, either before or during countdown.

secondary cosmic rays. Secondary emission in the atmosphere stimulated by primary cosmic rays.

selenocentric. Relating to the center of the moon; referring to the moon as a center.

selenographic. 1. Of or pertaining to the physical geography of the moon. 2. Specifically, referring to positions on the moon measured in latitude from the moon's equator and in longitude from a reference meridian.

sensible atmosphere. That part of the atmosphere that offers resistance to a body passing through it.

sensor. The component of an instrument that converts an input signal into a quantity which is measured by another part of the instrument. Also called "sensing element."

service tower = gantry scaffold.

shadowgraph. A picture or image in which steep density gradients in the flow about a body are made visible, the body itself being presented in silhouette. Short for "radiation shield"; "heat shield".

shock tube. A relatively long tube or pipe in which very brief high-speed gas flows are produced by the sudden release of gas at very high pressure into a low-pressure portion of the tube; the high-speed flow moves into the region of low pressure behind a shock wave.

The shock tube is used as a tool in the study of gases or as a kind of intermittent wind tunnel.

shot. An act or instance of firing a rocket, especially from the rocket's surface, as "the shot carried the rocket 200 miles."

sidereal. Of or pertaining to the stars.

solar radiation. The total electromagnetic radiation emitted by the sun.

solid propellant. Specifically, a rocket propellant in solid form, usually containing both fuel and oxidizer combined or mixed and formed into a monolithic (not powdered or granulated) grain. See rocket propellant and grain.

solid-propellant rocket engine. A rocket engine using a solid propellant. Such engines consist essentially of a combustion chamber containing the propellant, and a nozzle for the exhaust jet, although they often contain other components, as grids, liners, etc. See rocket engine.

sonic. 1. Aerodynamics: Of or pertaining to the speed of sound; that moves at the speed of sound, as in 'sonic flow'; designed to operate or perform at the speed of sound, as in "sonic leading edge." 2. Of or pertaining to sound, as in "sonic amplifier."

solar wind. A stream of protons constantly moving outward from the sun.

sonic boom. A noise caused by the shock wave that emanates from an aircraft or other object traveling in the atmosphere at or above the speed of sound.

sonic speed. The speed of sound; by extension, the speed of a body traveling at Mach 1.

Sound travels at different speeds through different mediums and at different speeds through any given medium under different conditions of temperature, etc. In the standard atmosphere at sea level, sonic speed is approximately 760 miles per hour.

sophisticated. Complex and intricate; making use of advanced art; requiring special skills to operate.

sounding. 1. In geophysics, any penetration of the natural environment for scientific observation. 2. In meteorology, same as upper-air observation. However, a common connotation is that of a single complete radiosonde observation.

sounding rocket. A rocket designed to explore the atmosphere within 4,000 miles of the earth's surface.

space. 1. Specifically, the part of the universe lying outside the limits of the earth's atmosphere. 2. More generally, the volume in which all spatial bodies, including the earth, move.

space-air vehicle. A vehicle that may be operated either within or above the sensible atmosphere.

spacecraft. Devices, manned and unmanned, which are designed to be placed into an orbit about the earth or into a trajectory to another celestial body.

space equivalent. A condition within the earth's atmosphere that is virtually identical, in terms of a particular function, with a condition in outer space.

For example, at 50,000 feet the low air pressure and the scarcity of oxygen create a condition, so far as respiration is concerned, that is equivalent to a condition in outer space where no appreciable oxygen is present; thus, a physiological space equivalent is present in the atmosphere.

space medicine. A branch of aerospace medicine concerned specifically with the health of persons who make, or expect to make, flights into space beyond the sensible atmosphere.

space probe. See probe.

space reddening. The observed reddening, or absorption of shorter wavelengths, of the light from distant celestial bodies caused by scattering by small particles in interstellar space. Compare red shift.

space simulator. A device which simulates some condition or conditions existing in space and used for testing equipment, or in training programs.

spatial. Pertaining to space.

specific impulse. A performance parameter of a rocket propellant, expressed in seconds, and equal to thrust (in pounds) divided by weight flow rate (in pounds per second). See thrust.

spectrometer. An instrument which measures some characteristics such as intensity, of electromagnetic radiation as a function of wavelength or frequency.

spectrum. 1. In physics, any series of energies arranged according to wavelength (or frequency); specifically, the series of images produced when a beam of radiant energy, such as sunlight, is dispersed by a prism or a reflecting grating. 2. Short for "electromagnetic spectrum" or for any part of it used for a specific purpose as the "radio spectrum" (10 kilocycles to 300,000 megacycles).

stage. A propulsion unit of a rocket, especially one unit of a multistage rocket, including its own fuel and tanks.

stage-and-a-half. A liquid-rocket propulsion unit of which only part falls away from the rocket vehicle during flight, as in the case of booster rockets falling away to leave the sustainer engine to consume remaining fuel.

standard atmosphere. A hypothetical vertical distribution of atmospheric temperature, pressure, and density which, by agreement, is taken to be representative of the atmosphere for purposes of pressure altimeter calibrations, aircraft performance calculations, aircraft and rocket design, ballistic tables, etc.

stationary orbit. An orbit in which an equatorial satellite revolves about the primary at the same angular rate as the primary rotates on its axis. From the primary, the satellite thus appears to be stationary over a point on the primary.

subatomic particle. A component of an atom, such as an electron, a proton, a meson, etc.

subsonic. In aerodynamics, dealing with speeds less than the speed of sound (see sonic speed), as in *"subsonic aerodynamics."*

sun*.* A relatively dark area on the surface of the sun, consisting of a dark central umbra and a surrounding penumbra that is intermediate in brightness between the umbra and the surrounding photosphere.

sunspot cycle. A periodic variation in the number and area of sunspots with an average length of 11.1 years, but varying between about 7 and 17 years.

supersonic. Pertaining to speeds greater than the speed of sound. Compare ultrasonic.

sustainer engine. An engine that maintains the velocity of a missile or rocket vehicle, once it has achieved its programed velocity through use of a booster engine.

synchronous satellite. An equatorial west-to-east satellite orbiting the earth at an altitude of 22,300 statute miles at which altitude it makes one revolution in 24 hours, synchronous with the earth's rotation.

synergic curve. A curve plotted for the ascent of a rocket, space-air vehicle, or space vehicle calculated to give the vehicle an optimum economy in fuel with an optimum velocity.

This curve, plotted to minimize air resistance, starts off vertically, but bends towards the horizontal between 20 and 60 miles altitude.

tektite. A small glassy body containing no crystals, probably of meteoritic origin, and bearing no antecedent relation to the geological formation in which it occurs.

Tektites are found in certain large areas called "strewn fields." They are named as minerals with the suffix "ite," as "australite," found in Australia; "billitonite," "indochinite," and "rizalite," found in Southeast Asia; "bediasite" from Texas, and "moldavite" from Bohemia and Moravia.

telemetry. The science of measuring a quantity or quantities, transmitting the measured value to a distant station, and there interpreting, indicating, or recording the quantities measured.

terminator. The line separating illuminated and dark portions of a nonluminous body, as the moon.

terrestrial. Pertaining to the earth.

thermal. Pertaining to heat or temperature.

thermodynamic. Pertaining to the flow of heat or to thermodynamics.

thermodynamics. The study of the relationships between heat and other forms of energy.

thermonuclear. Pertaining to a nuclear reaction that is triggered by particles of high thermal energy.

thrust. 1. The pushing force developed by an aircraft engine or a rocket engine. 2. Specifically, in rocketry, the product of propellant mass flow rate and exhaust velocity relative to the vehicle.

topside sounder. A satellite designed to measure ion concentration in the ionosphere from above the ionosphere.

tracking. The process of following the movement of a satellite or rocket by radar, radio, and photographic observations.

trajectory. In general, the path traced by any body, as a rocket, moving as a result of externally applied forces.

Trajectory is loosely used to mean "flight path" or "orbit."

transducer. A device capable of being actuated by energy from one or more transmission systems or media and of supplying related energy to one or more other transmission systems or media, as a microphone, a thermocouple, etc.

transfer orbit. In interplanetary travel an elliptical trajectory tangent to the orbits of both the departure planet and the target planet.

transit. 1. The passage of a celestial body across a celestial meridian; usually called "meridian transit." 2. The apparent passage of a celestial body across the face of another celestial body or across any point, area, or line.

translunar. Of or pertaining to space outside the moon's orbit about the earth.

transponder. A combined receiver and transmitter whose function is to transmit signals automatically when triggered by an interrogating signal.

T-time. Any specific time, minus or plus, as referenced to "zero," or "launch" time, during a countdown sequence that is intended to result in the firing of a rocket propulsion unit that launches a rocket vehicle or missile.

ullage. The amount that a container, such as a fuel tank, lacks of being full.

ultrasonic. Of or pertaining to frequencies above those that affect the human ear, i.e., more than 20,000 vibrations per second.

The term "ultrasonic" may be used as a modifier to indicate a device or system intended to operate at an ultrasonic frequency.

Although "supersonic" was formerly used in acoustics synonymously with "ultrasonic," this usage is now rare.

ultraviolet radiation. Electromagnetic radiation shorter in wavelength than visible radiation but longer than X-rays; roughly, radiation in the wavelength interval between 10 and 4,000 angstroms.

Ultraviolet radiation from the sun is responsible for many complex photochemical reactions characteristic of the upper atmosphere, e.g., the formation of the ozone layer through ultraviolet dissociation of oxygen molecules followed by recombination to form ozone.

umbilical cord. Any of the servicing electrical or fluid lines between the ground or a tower and an upright rocket missile or vehicle before the launch. Often shortened to "umbilical."

upper-air observation. A measurement of atmospheric conditions aloft, above the effective range of a surface weather observation. Also called "sounding," "upper-air sounding."

Van Allen Belt, Van Allen Radiation Belt, Van Allen Radiation Region. (For James A. Van Allen, 1915– .) The zone of high-intensity radiation surrounding the earth beginning at altitudes of approximately 500 miles.

vehicle. Specifically, a structure, machine, or device, such as an aircraft or rocket, designed to carry a burden through air or space; more restrictively, a rocket craft.

This word has acquired its specific meaning owing to the need for a term to embrace all flying craft, including aircraft and rockets.

vernier engine. A rocket engine of small thrust used primarily to obtain a fine adjustment in the velocity and trajectory of a ballistic missile or space vehicle just after the thrust cutoff of the last propulsion engine, and used secondarily to add thrust to a booster or sustainer engine. Also called "vernier rocket."

visible radiation. Electromagnetic radiation lying within the wavelength interval to which the human eye is sensitive, which is from approximately 0.4 to 0.7 micron (4,000 to 7,000 angstroms). This portion of the electromagnetic spectrum is bounded on the short-wavelength end by ultraviolet radiation, and on the long-wavelength end by infrared radiation.

weight. The force with which an earthbound body is attracted toward the earth.

weightlessness. 1. A condition in which no acceleration, whether of gravity or other force can be detected by an observer within the system in question. 2. A condition in which gravitational and other external forces acting on a body produce no stress, either internal or external, in the body.

Any object falling freely in a vacuum is weightless, thus an unaccelerated satellite orbiting the earth is "weightless" although gravity affects its orbit. Weightlessness can be produced within the atmosphere in aircraft flying a parabolic flight path.

whistler. A radiofrequency electromagnetic signal sometimes generated by lightning discharges.

This signal apparently propagates along a geomagnetic line of force, and often "bounces" several times between the Northern and Southern Hemispheres. Its name derives from the sound heard on radio receivers.

X-ray. Electromagnetic radiation of very short wavelength, lying within the wavelength interval of 0.1 to 100 angstroms (between gamma rays and ultraviolet radiation). Also called "X-radiation," "Roentgen ray."

X-rays penetrate various thicknesses of all solids and they act upon photographic plates in the same manner as light. Secondary X-rays are produced whenever X-rays are absorbed by a substance, in the case of absorption by a gas, this results in ionization.

yaw. 1. The lateral rotational or oscillatory movement of an aircraft, rocket, or the like about a transverse axis. 2. The amount of this movement; i.e., the angle of yaw.

zero g = weightlessness.

Printed in Germany
by Amazon Distribution
GmbH, Leipzig